TI

Trans P

CW00421025

ACCOMMODATION AND VISITOR GUIDE

EXCELLENT BOOKS

EXCELLENT BOOKS
94 BRADFORD ROAD
WAKEFIELD
WEST YORKSHIRE WF1 2AE
TEL / FAX: (01924) 315147
E-mail: richard@excellentbooks.co.uk
Website: www.excellentbooks.co.uk

First Published January 2001

ISBN 1-901464-09-1

Whilst the author has cycled and researched the route for the purposes of this guide, no responsibility can be accepted for any unforeseen circumstances encountered whilst following it. The publisher would, however, welcome information regarding any material changes and problems encountered.

Front cover photos, clockwise from top left:
Aire & Calder Canal towpath, south of Leeds
Manchester Ship Canal, Wilderspool / Stockton Heath
The Humber Bridge
Upper Don Trail, near Wortley
Frontispiece: TPT running alongside River Don near Sprotbrough

Printed in Great Britain by:
FM Repro Ltd.
Repro House, 69 Lumb Lane
Roberttown
Liversedge
West Yorkshire WF15 7NB

CONTENTS

Liverpool waterfront (section 1 - city centre spur)

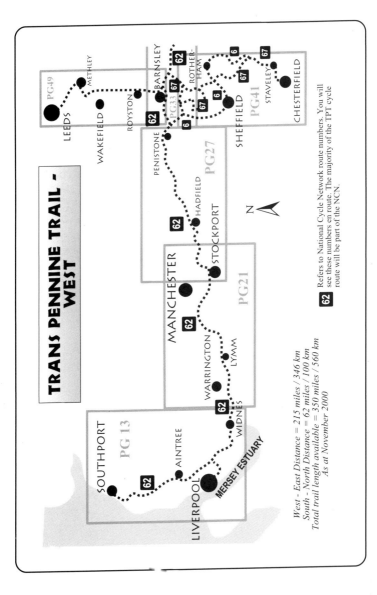

TRANS PENNINE TRAIL - WEST

West - East Distance = 215 miles / 346 km
South - North Distance = 62 miles / 100 km
Total trail length available = 350 miles / 560 km
As at November 2000

62 Refers to National Cycle Network route numbers. You will see these numbers en route. The majority of the TPT cycle route will be part of the NCN.

SOUTHPORT — PG 13
AINTREE
LIVERPOOL
MERSEY ESTUARY
WIDNES
WARRINGTON
LYMM
MANCHESTER
STOCKPORT — PG21
HADFIELD
PENISTONE — PG27
LEEDS — PG49
METHLEY
WAKEFIELD
ROYSTON
BARNSLEY
ROTHERHAM
PG33
SHEFFIELD — PG41
STAVELEY
CHESTERFIELD

N

4

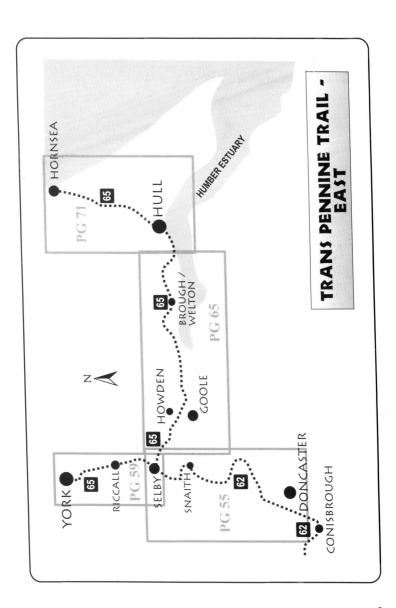

TRANS PENNINE TRAIL - EAST

HORNSEA

HULL

HUMBER ESTUARY

65

PG 71

BROUGH / WELTON

65

PG 65

N

HOWDEN

GOOLE

65

YORK

RICCALL

65

PG 59

SELBY

SNAITH

62

PG 55

DONCASTER

62

CONISBROUGH

5

INTRODUCTION

WHAT IS THE TRANS PENNINE TRAIL (TPT)?

• The first multi-user long distance route in the country.
• A recreation and transport route, currently for walkers and cyclists, with sections also available for horse riders and people using wheelchairs and pushchairs.
• A coast to coast route, linking the ports of Liverpool and Hull with connections to the seaside resorts of Southport on the Irish Sea and Hornsea on the North Sea.
• It links major towns and cities across the North including Leeds, Wakefield, Barnsley, York, Selby, Manchester, Doncaster, Rotherham, Sheffield and Chesterfield.
• 215 miles (346km) coast to coast, with a total trail length of 350 miles (560km).
• A very large percentage of the route avoids roads, using disused railway lines, riversides, canal towpaths and cross-country paths.
• Part of the National Cycle Network, which will total more than 10,000 miles by 2005.
• Developed by a unique partnership of 26 local authorities across the North, with the project office based in Barnsley, South Yorkshire.
• It is the first designated European Long Distance Route for walkers in the country, linking the west of Ireland with Bulgaria and Turkey. (Long distance route E8).

OPENING TIMETABLE AND USER GROUPS

By early 2001 most of the TPT will be signed and available for use. The full route is for walkers and cyclists with long stretches also for horse riders. Many miles have relatively easy access suitable for some trail users with physical disabilities or families with young children. Efforts will continue beyond 2001 to continually improve and enhance the trail for all users across the country.

FRIENDS OF THE TRANS PENNINE TRAIL

The Friends of the Trans Pennine Trail is a voluntary body of people who want to get the most out of the trail and see it succeed. They help by lobbying and campaigning, practical assistance, supporting the trail project team, promoting the TPT and operating a system of voluntary trail stewards.

For further details contact the Friends' Secretary:

Richard Haynes, 32 Dalebrook Court, Sheffield S10 3PQ (0114) 2305358
e-mail: richard@haynes1.fsnet.co.uk

ROUTE FEATURES - A SUMMARY

Landscape features, west to east:

Formby / Ainsdale Hills - unusual dune landscape, with sands still accumulating as the sea retreats.

Mersey Estuary - Liverpool spur finishes at the Pierhead on the Mersey. The main route comes alongside the Mersey near Widnes, passing beneath the spectacular Runcorn Bridge.

River Mersey South Manchester. Flood plain and gravel pit provide wildlife havens.

Central Pennines - Dark Peak area. Pass down Longdendale, flanked by high, brooding Shining Clough Moss and Highstone Rocks.

East Yorkshire Plain Flat, open countryside, crossed by drainage ditches and punctuated by graceful church spires.

Humber Estuary - Massive! Contains water from a fifth of the country's rivers.

Man-made features, west to east:

Southport Architecture - Beautiful arcades on Lord Street plus pier and miles of open sand.

Liverpool - Anglican and Roman Catholic cathedrals plus Liver Building.

Manchester Ship Canal - 36 miles long (the route uses only a short section). Little-used by ships nowadays but still spectacular.

Yorkshire's Industrial Heritage - mining site reclamation at the Earth Centre and throughout much of the South and West Yorkshire area.

Conisbrough Castle - Impressive ruins with 90 feet high, 12th century keep.

Sheffield - former 'steel city', with a small portion of the famous knife blade industry remaining.

Leeds - financial centre of the North, once a centre of the wool trade. Fine Victorian buildings including the Cornmarket, food market and Town Hall. Tetleys' brewery museum and Royal Armouries. Thwaites Mill Industrial Museum on TPT canal section, south of centre.

York - Superlative Minster and rich historical legacy with a wealth of fascinating buildings and outstanding city walls.

Stunningly graceful **Abbeys and Minsters** of East Yorks - e.g. Selby & Howden.

Stunning **Humber Bridge**, with its huge single-span central section.

Hull's Docks Britain's third largest port after London and Liverpool. Infilled docks now form part of city centre. Interesting Old Town area with Maritime Museum and William Wilberforce (anti-slavery campaigner) connections.

SIGNIFICANT TRAFFIC-FREE SECTIONS (Railpath and canal towpath)

TRAIL	FROM	TO	KM	CHAP.
Cheshire Lines	Ainsdale	Maghull	16	1
Liverpool Loop Line	Aintree	Halewood	16	1
St Helens Canal	Spike Island	Warrington	10	2
Broadheath - Lymm Railpath	Altrincham	Lymm	14	2
River Mersey Path	Sale	Stockport	15	2
Longdendale	Hadfield Station	Windle Edge	10.5	3
Upper Don	Dunford Bridge	Wortley	17	3
Dove Valley	Silkstone Common	Wombwell	12	4
Five Weirs Walk	Meadowhall	Sheffield	7	5
Beighton - Staveley	Beighton	Staveley	9	5
Chesterfield Canal	Staveley	Chesterfield	8	5
Aire & Calder Navigation	Wood Row Mickletown	Leeds	10	6
York - Selby	Selby	York	24	6
Hull - Hornsea	Hull	Hornsea	21	10

MAPS AND TRANSPORT

Three official map guides are due out spring 2001 to coincide with the official trail launch. They will show all route options for walkers, cyclists and horse riders. Together with this guide they provide all the information trail users need, along the whole length of the trail. The maps are available separately or as a set from the Trans Pennine Trail Office (see below) or from all good bookshops;
Trans Pennine Trail West Irish Sea to Pennines
Trans Pennine Trail Central Derbyshire and Yorkshire
Trans Pennine Trail East Yorkshire to North Sea

Much of the TPT is well served by rail. The two main exceptions where train transport becomes more distant are the Longdendale Trail area and the Hull-Hornsea section. Bikes usually cost £3 per trip on inter-city journeys and space must be reserved. For details about carrying bikes on local services ask the local train operating company about their policy. Buses are handy for walkers but will only take folding bikes. Details of 'bike-bus' services and ferry connections are given in the 'Information File' sections at the end of the relevant chapters.

National Train Information 08457 484950 or www.thetrainline.com
Local Travel Information (buses, trains and trams)
Merseyside (0151) 2367676   8 until 8 daily
Greater Manchester (0161) 2287811   8 until 8 daily
Derbyshire (01332) 292200   7 until 8 daily
South Yorkshire (01709) 515151   8 until 6 daily
West Yorkshire (0113) 2457676   8 until 7 daily
East Yorkshire (01482) 222222   (buses only)

USEFUL CONTACT ADDRESSES

Trans Pennine Trail Office Barnsley Metropolitan Borough Council, Central Offices, Kendray Street, Barnsley S70 2TN Tel.(01226) 772574
e-mail: transpenninetrail@barnsley.gov.uk
website: www.transpenninetrail.org.uk
Local Authorities have developed and look after the trail in their area. See phone book or enquire at TPT office for details of relevant local authority.
Ramblers Association 1/5 Wandsworth Road, London SW8 2XX
(020) 73398500
Sustrans 35 King Street, Bristol BS1 4DZ (0117) 9290888
Cyclists Touring Club Cotterell House, 69 Meadrow, Godalming, Surrey GU7 3HS (01483) 417217
British Horse Society Stoneleigh Deer Park, Kenilworth, Warks CV8 2XZ (01926) 707700 *website:* www.bhs.org.uk
Camping & Caravanning Club Greenfields House, Westwood Way, Coventry CV4 8JH (024) 76694995
Full Tourist Offices details are given in relevant chapters under **INFORMATION FILE**.

Trans Pennine Trail

USER CODE

The Trans Pennine Trail is a route for walkers, cyclists and horseriders. They often share the same route and occasionally the path is divided for different users. Currently some sections are not available to horses and some may be difficult for people using wheelchairs or pushchairs though much is fully accessible.

To keep everybody safe and happy...................

Every effort has been made to create a route suitable for all permitted users, but enjoyment of the Trans Pennine Trail relies on everybody showing consideration to each other:

- where different paths, or sides of the path are signed for different user groups - please keep to yours
- if in a group, please do not walk or ride across the whole width of the path, leave space for others to pass you easily
- take great care where the Trans Pennine Trail crosses or follows roads
- take all your litter home and be careful with cigarette ends due to risk of fire

- dog owners - please clean up after your pet - dog mess spoils the trail and adjacent areas for other people and poses health risks
- keep close control of your dog - preferably on a short lead, especially where farm animals are present

- use only sections of the trail where horses are allowed
- do not use the trail unless you can control your horse - you may encounter walkers, people using wheelchairs and scooters, cyclists, dogs and bridges over road, rail and water
- do not canter or gallop on shared sections of the trail
- please avoid damaging trail surfaces and don't ride on the grassed central dividing strip between paths

- warn others when you approach from behind so you do not startle people as you pass by - call politely or use a bell / hooter
- slow down when approaching other users who are unpredictable, particularly children or animals. Remember too, some people may be deaf or hard of hearing
- helmets and high visibility clothing will add to your safety

- must not use this route for racing competitions or speed trials
- on canal towpaths - read and abide by the British Waterways code for cyclists
- please be prepared to dismount occasionally - on steep access ramps, or on limited sections (such as restricted width bridges)
- where the trail is a designated bridleway, cyclists should give way to other users
- be careful with your speed - especially on slopes or where visibility ahead is limited

Everybody - Please enjoy the Trans Pennine Trail and help others to do so too!

IMPORTANT

Please note that the route maps shown at the beginning of each chapter throughout this guide are schematic only. For actual user details and navigation on the ground please refer to the official TPT maps detailed on page 9.

1 SOUTHPORT - WIDNES

Section Distance 29 miles / 47km

The Route From Southport head through the beautiful dunes of the Birkdale Hills then inland and onto the Cheshire Lines, through flat market gardening country towards Maghull. Track, canal towpath and minor roads link to the Liverpool Loop Line, like the Cheshire Lines, a disused railway. Out of the Liverpool suburbs you are onto minor roads through pretty Hale village before spectacular off-road sections by the Mersey estuary around the Widnes-Runcorn bridge. Walkers and cyclists are separated for only a very short while, in the dune area south of Southport.

A 7.5 mile spur leads off the Liverpool Loop Line near Childwall. Attractive suburbs and parks lead into Liverpool centre, passing the stunning Anglican Cathedral to finish in the famous dock area with linking ferries to the Isle of Man and Dublin. This uses mainly minor roads and cycle lanes with shared use paths through Sefton and Princes Parks. Full details begin on page 16.

HOTELS & GUESTHOUSES

Carlton Lodge Hotel, 43 Bath Street, Southport PR9 0DP (01704) 542290 benvale@which.net £20-22. ♦♦♦♦ 3s1d6f March-October Dist. 1.5 miles

Edendale Hotel, 83 Avondale Road North, Southport PR9 0NE (01704) 530718 www.edendalehotel.co.uk £19.50-27.50. 2s4d2f Dist. 2 miles

Elsinore Guest House, 43 King Street, Southport PR8 1LG (01704) 532766. £15.00 approx. Dist. 1.25 miles

Sidbrook Hotel, 14 Talbot Street, Southport PR8 1HP (01704) 530608. sidbrookhotel@tesco.net £19.50-22.50. ♦♦♦ 2t 6d Dist. 1 mile.

Whitworth Falls Hotel, 16 Lathom Road, Southport PR9 0JH (01704) 530074. whitworthfalls@rapid.co.uk / www.whitworthfallshotel.co.uk £19-25 **R** 13 rooms Dist. 2 miles Small fee.

There shouldn't be any problem finding accommodation in Southport at short notice outside of the busiest of peak seasons; much of it is on **King Street**, **Bath Street**, **Bold Street** and **Duke Street**.

FOR ACCOMMODATION SYMBOLS KEY SEE INSIDE COVER

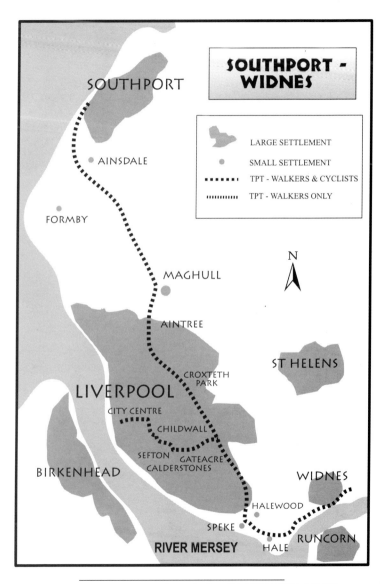

SOUTHPORT - WIDNES

LARGE SETTLEMENT

SMALL SETTLEMENT

TPT - WALKERS & CYCLISTS

TPT - WALKERS ONLY

SOUTHPORT

AINSDALE

FORMBY

N

MAGHULL

AINTREE

ST HELENS

CROXTETH PARK

LIVERPOOL

CITY CENTRE

CHILDWALL

SEFTON CALDERSTONES

GATEACRE

BIRKENHEAD

WIDNES

HALEWOOD

SPEKE

RUNCORN

HALE

RIVER MERSEY

7 Church Avenue, Aintree, Liverpool L9 4SG (0151) 5258166. £14. **R.**
🛏 2t ⑥ **Dist.** 0.25 miles

Parkland, 38 Coachmans Drive, Croxteth Park, Liverpool L12 0HX (0151) 2591417.
£20. **R** 🛏 1d1t 📷 ⬚ ⑥ ✗ **Dist.** 1.25 miles

Gateacre Hall Hotel, The Nook, Halewood Road, Gateacre, Liverpool L25 5PG
(0151) 4286322 Fax (0151) 4284302. £27-36 (cheaper price applies at weekends).
★★★ 🛏 20d/s 📷 📷 ⬚ ▼ **Dist.** 0.25 miles Residential bar.

Church End Farm, 5 Church End, Hale L24 4AX (0151) 4254273.
📧 churchendfarm@talk21.com £20. **R.** 🛏 2s4d 📷 ⬚ ▼ ⑥ ✗
Dist. 0.25 miles

Motel Olympia, Tanhouse Lane, Widnes WA8 0RR (0151) 4246355. £12.50-
18.50. 🛏 13s24d 📷 ⬚ Laundry service. **Dist.** 0.75 miles

Victoria Guesthouse, 2 Fairfield Road, Widnes WA8 6SE (0151) 4241048.
£15. 🛏 2 📷 ⬚ ⑥ ✗ Self-catering facilities. **Dist.** 1.25 miles

HOSTELS & CAMPSITES

Willowbank Holiday Home and Touring Park, Coastal Road, Ainsdale,
Southport PR8 3ST (01704) 571566. Approx £4 per person per night. Open
March - early January. Toilets, showers and laundry facilities. Mini-market type
shop nearby.

Thatched cottage at Hale (section 1)

FOOD & DRINK

Plenty of food and drink outlets in **Southport**.
National Wildflower Centre opening April 2001, next to the trail, just before
the spur off to the city centre. Toilets and cafe outside of admission paygate.
See below for details.
Gateacre Park Drive, just off the Liverpool Loop Line near the link to Liverpool
city centre and pier head, has take-aways, restaurants and a nearby pub.
Childe of Hale Pub, Church End, Hale Village. Bar snacks. (0151) 4252954
Wellington pub on TPT in Hale. Hale Post Office sells snacks.

ATTRACTIONS

Southport Elegant seaside resort. Grand architecture on Lord Street.
Attractive **Marine Lake** and **Pier** area front onto miles of open sands.
Museum in Botanic Gardens at Churchtown holds impressive collection of
Victoriana (01704) 227547. **Model Village** is a family favourite, recently opened
after closure of previous model village (01704) 214266. The **Pier** is one of the
longest in the UK and was being restored with lottery money at the time of
writing.
Croxteth Country Park Edwardian country house over 500 acres of parkland.
Children's farm and miniature railway. (0151) 2285311. Refreshments / toilets.
National Wildflower Centre, Court Hey Park. Visitor attraction opening April
2001. Working nursery in 35 acres of open space. Seasonal opening. (0151) 7371819.
Hale Village inn sign depicts John Middleton, reputed 9ft 3 inch giant who
defeated James I's wrestling champion in 17th century. Pretty village with 18th
century church. Ruins of Hale Hall to west of village. Unusual 'Childe of Hale',
sculptured from a tree stump on road to estuary front and lighthouse.
Pickerings Pasture Local nature reserve with wild flower meadows and views across
the River Mersey. Hale Marshes birdwatching area. Ranger centre and toilets.
Widnes Centre of chemical industry. Spectacular views from Widnes-Runcorn
Bridge, where St Helens Canal and Manchester Ship Canal join Mersey estuary.

INFORMATION FILE

Tourist Information
Southport: 112 Lord Street (01704) 533333.
Widnes: Municipal Buildings, Kingsway (0151) 4242061.
Runcorn: 57 Church Street (01928) 576776.
Hospital Southport & Formby General, Town Lane, Southport (01704) 547471
Banks All main high street banks in Southport and Widnes centres.
🚲 **Re Cycles** 272 Liverpool Road, Southport (01704) 567351
NE Mosscrop 78 Bispham Road, Southport (01704) 228805
Aintree Bike Centre 336 Longmoor Lane, Aintree, Liverpool (0151) 5217821
Bike King 277 East Prestcott Road, Knotty Ash, Liverpool (0151) 4752882
Crays Cycles Ltd 207 Liverpool Road North, Maghull (0151) 5269566
John Geddes Cycles 43 Widnes Road, Widnes (0151) 4207797

HOTELS & GUESTHOUSES - LIVERPOOL CENTRE SPUR

Real McCoy Guesthouse, 126 Childwall Park Avenue, Liverpool L16 0JH
(0151) 7227116. £23-25. ♦♦♦ ⤳1s2d 🍴 · ⍓ **Dist.** 0.25 miles

Somersby, 57 Green Lane, Menlove Gardens, Calderstones, Liverpool L18 2EP
Tel/fax (0151) 7227549. £19-22.50 ♦♦♦ 🍴 · 🚲 ✗ **Dist.** 0.25 miles

Blenheim Lodge, 37 Aigburth Drive, Sefton Park, Liverpool L17 4JE
(0151) 7277380 Fax (0151) 7275833 ▄theblenheimguesthouse@BTinternet.com
£16.50-19.50. ♦♦♦ ⤳ 16 s/d/f 🍴 🍴 · ⍓ 🚲 **Dist.** 0.25 miles.
Residential bar.

Solna Hotel, 4 Croxteth Drive,Sefton Park, Liverpool L17 3AD (0151) 7343398
Fax (0151) 7344840 ▄ www.feathers.uk.com £22-29. ★★★ ⤳ 20 rooms
🍴 🍴 🚲 **Dist.** 0.25 miles. Residential bar.

Liverpool University c/o Conference Services, Greenbank Conference Park,
Berby & Rathbone Hall, North Mossley Hill Road, Liverpool L18 8BH
(0151) 7946440 Fax (0151) 7946520 ▄confoff@liv.ac.uk / www.merseyworld.com/liv-conf/
£20.90 ⤳ 400 single rooms and 160 self-catering apartments at two campuses.
Only available over two periods in spring and summer. Call for more details of
exact services and availability dates. **Dist.** Campuses near Sefton Park and city
centre.

Aachen Hotel, 89-91 Mount Pleasant, Liverpool L3 5TB (0151) 7093477 Phone/
fax (0151) 7091126 & (0151) 7093633. £20-26. ♦♦♦ ⤳ sdtf 🍴 🍴 ·
⍓ 🚲 Bar games / pool. **Dist.** 0.5 miles from Liverpool spur, near city centre.

HOSTELS & CAMPSITES - LIVERPOOL CENTRE SPUR

YHA Liverpool International, 25 Tabley Street, Off Wapping, Liverpool L1 8EE
(0151) 7098888 ▄liverpool@yha.org.uk £15.85-19. ⤳ 100 beds. Mainly 4-
6 bed rooms and 4 doubles (all en-suite) 🍴 🍴 · ⍓ 🚲 **Dist.** 0.25 miles.
Self-catering facilities.

FOOD & DRINK - LIVERPOOL CENTRE SPUR

Childwall Abbey (pub) Good range of beers and reasonably priced food (0151)
7225293.
Snack bar in centre of **Sefton Park**.
Chinatown, with a good choice of restaurants, approaching Liverpool centre is
particularly interesting,

Approaching the towering Anglican cathedral in Liverpool (section 1 - centre spur)

ATTRACTIONS - LIVERPOOL CENTRE SPUR

7 miles of docks still line the estuary front of what was once the premier Atlantic port of Europe. Shipping declined,leaving decay in its wake but much of the city has been regenerated. Outstanding cultural, architectural and visitor highlights are:

1. Anglican Cathedral Incredible views from 331ft tower. Completed 1904-1978. Stunning building sitting on wooded crag. (0151) 7096271.
2. Chinatown Good selection of restaurants.
3. Roman Catholic Cathedral Circular building from 1960s. Beautiful lantern tower with stained glass. (0151) 7099222.
4. St George's Hall Imposing neo-classical building with luxurious interior. For limited seasonal opening times call (0151) 7072391.
5. Liverpool Museum & Planetarium From natural history to outer space. (0151) 4784399.
6. Albert Dock Area Numerous attractions in converted warehouse include: **Beatles Story** (0151) 7091963 **Tate Gallery**, largest collection of contemporary art outside London (0151) 7027400 **Merseyside Maritime Museum** showing city's history of sugar and slave trading, White Star and Cunard liner businesses and the vast 19th century emigration via the port (0151) 4784499.
7. Museum of Liverpool Life Mersey culture and local people (0151) 4784080.
8. Mersey Ferries 50 minute cruise leaving from in front of famous landmark of **Liver Building**. (0151) 6390609.
9. Western Approaches Original World War II underground H.Q. 50,000 sq ft of operations rooms. (0151) 2272008.

INFORMATION FILE - LIVERPOOL CENTRE SPUR

Tourist Information Atlantic Pavilion, Albert Dock (0151) 7088854
Hospital Liverpool Royal Hospital, Prescot Street (0151) 7062000
Banks All main high street banks with cashpoints in central shopping area of Liverpool, just to the north of the TPT route along lower Duke Street.
Transport Seacat services to Isle of Man and Dublin leave from Prince's stage, north of Liver Building. 08705 523523. Ferry service to Dublin (01532) 779090
⚒ **Abbey Cycles** 44 Childwall Abbey Road, Childwall, Liverpool (0151) 7220999
Rose Lane Cycles 27 Rose Lane, Mossley Hill, Liverpool (0151) 7245240
Liverpool Cycle Centre 9-13 Berry Street, Liverpool (0151) 7088819

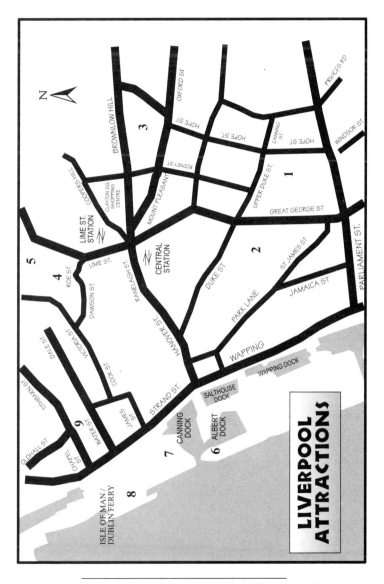

2 WIDNES - STOCKPORT

Section Distance 32miles / 52km

The Route At Widnes you pick up the St. Helens Canal towpath with fine views over the Mersey Estuary where it begins to narrow. Crossing the Mersey south of Warrington leads to a short but spectacular section alongside the Manchester Ship Canal. A 9 mile / 15km section of disused railpath then crosses the Cheshire plain and enters the Trafford district of Greater Manchester. Although this area is often associated with chemicals production the trail largely avoids areas of heavy industry and passes close to such gems as Grappenhall and Lymm. Along the Mersey Valley, south of central Manchester, and through Stockport the route uses a wide-ranging mixture of paths (some alongside the River Mersey) and a variety of roads. Finally you have the option of going through Stockport centre or taking a more northern option towards Hyde. There are several walkers' options along the Mersey Valley section.

HOTELS & GUESTHOUSES

Maples Hotel, 11 Longdin Street, Latchford, Warrington WA4 1PW (01925) 637752. £15-20. 1s1d3t1f (• by arrangement) **Dist.** 0.5 miles

Imperial Hotel, Bewsey Road, Warrington (01925) 637255. £16-22.50. ♦♦ 4s1t1tr   **Dist.** 1 mile. Breakfast £4.50 extra.

Brook Cottage, Kay Lane, Lymm WA13 0TN (01925) 755530. £25. 1t1s   **Dist.** 0.5 miles

Rams Head Pub, Grappenhall Village, Grappenhall, Warrington WA4 3EP (01925) 262814 davidcross1@lineone.net £20-40. 1s2t   •   **Dist.** 0.5 miles. Also see Food & Drink entry.

Bollington Hall Farm, Little Bollington, Altrincham WA14 4TJ (0161) 9281760. £18. **R.** (Notice required) **Dist.** 2.5 miles.

Belvedere Guesthouse, 58 Barrington Road, Altrincham WA14 1HY (0161) 9415996. £20-28. 4s/d •   **Dist.** 1.25 miles By arrangement.

Bollin Hotel, 58 Manchester Road, Altrincham WA14 4PJ (0161) 9282390. £18-22. 5s5d/t **Dist.** 1 mile. Near Altrincham centre (pubs & restaurants)

Old Mill Hotel, 2 Barrington Road, Altrincham WA14 1HH (0161) 9282960. £20-25. •   **Dist** 1.25 miles

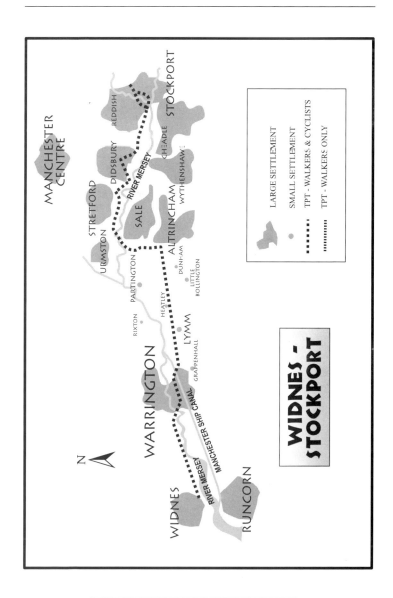

Brooklands Luxury Lodge, 208 Marsland Road, Sale M33 3NE
(0161) 9733283. £23-26. ♦♦♦♦ ⤵ 5s4d 🍽 🚲 **Dist.** 1.5 miles. Jacuzzi.

Green Gables Guest House, 152 Barlow Moor Road, West Didsbury M20 2UT
(0161) 4455365. £18 (student discount). **R.** ⤵ 25 rooms s/d/tr/f 🍽 🚲
Dist. 0.5 miles.

Palatine Hotel, 88 Palatine Road, West Didsbury M20 3JW (0161) 4462222
£18-29.50. **R.** ⤵ 11s10d5t 🍷 **Dist:** 1 mile

Northumbria House, 35 Corbar Road, Stockport SK2 6EP (0161) 4834000.
£18-20. ⤵ 2 rooms 🍽 (• by arrangement) 🍷 🚲 **Dist.** 1.5 miles
Non-smoking.

HOSTELS & CAMPSITES

Hollybank Caravan Park, Warburton Bridge Road, Rixton, Warrington WA3 6HU
(0161) 7752842. • 🍷 🚲 ✗ **Dist.** 2 miles. Toilets, showers and small
shop.
For **very basic accommodation** Scout troop premises at **East Didsbury**, 0.5
miles from the trail are available. Toilets and mattresses. Phone David Mott on
(0161) 4310277 for more details. No set cost but donations welcome.

Fiddlers Ferry Tavern on the St. Helens Canal (section 2)

FOOD & DRINK

Ferry Tavern alongside trail on St Helens Canal. Meals Mon-Sat 12-2 & 6-9. Bar snacks / full menu. Boddingtons, Courage, Ruddles. Over 250 whiskies! (01925) 791117

Stockton Heath All the usual high street facilities plus a selection of restaurants and pubs. Just off trail up busy road. Morrisons next to trail at Stockton Heath.

Rams Head, Grappenhall village. Food all day. Sandwiches to a la carte. Boddingtons and Greenalls beers. (01925) 262814.

Lymm Excellent range of shops and cafes from fish and chips to upmarket bistros. Supermarket, grocers and plenty of pubs.

Heatley Green Dragon and **Railway** pubs do food. **La Boheme** French restaurant opposite Green Dragon, around £10-15 per head (01925) 753657.

Two pubs in **Dunham Woodhouses**, both doing food.

Dunham Massey Hall Historic house has cafe/restaurant and toilets. 1 mile from route. See attractions below for more details.

Sale Water Park Deckers Restaurant plus small cafe at visitor centre. Toilets. See Attractions overleaf for more details on the water park.

Row of convenience shops on Merseybank Avenue near **Chorlton Water Park**. See Attractions overleaf for more details.

Church Road, Northenden. Just off trail before it passes under M63 (exit at **Tatton Arms** which also does food).Traditional fish & chips. Also take-aways and pubs around the B5167 (Palatine Road) as it passes through Northenden. Pubs and eateries in **Didsbury** centre.

Stockport Cafes and restaurants plus Tuesday, Friday and Saturday markets.

ATTRACTIONS

Widnes-Runcorn Bridge Impressive local landmark.

St Helens Canal Significant traffic-free trail utilises the towpath of this canal that joins the Manchester Ship Canal with the Mersey estuary. One of Britain's oldest canals. **Spike Island** at the start of the canal has a visitor centre and toilets. Massive cooling towers of Fiddlers Ferry power station a notable landmark on this section. Good views across the Mersey Estuary on the later sections.

Catalyst National museum of the chemical industry at the western end of the canal, near **Spike Island** (visitor centre and toilets). Good views from top floor (0151) 4201121.

Manchester Ship Canal Built to link the city's once great textile industry to the sea. It allows sea-going vessels of almost 15,000 tons to sail almost to the city centre. The TPT uses a short section alongside the canal at south Warrington. For details of Saturday cruises along the canal in summer ring (0151) 3301444.

Grappenhall Modern commuter suburbs hide quaint old village. Cobbled street, church and two pubs (see above).

Lymm Charming village with unusual stocks and market cross on rock outcrop in centre. Attractive rocky gorge runs through village with artificial lake. Bridgwater canal also runs through centre; one of the earliest canals, built by the Duke of Bridgwater to exploit his coal reserves.

Dunham Massey Hall Georgian house with superb gardens, 1 mile from the route. National Trust property. Seasonal opening (0161) 9411025.

Sale Water Park Various water sports, from jet skiing to canoes, on this sizeable lake south of the River Mersey. (0161) 9123410/11/12.

Chorlton Water Park Large lakes in former gravel pits. Ideal for anglers, boaters and ornithologists. Toilets (suitable for disabled users). (0161) 8815639.

Wythenshawe Hall, Northenden. Half-timbered 16th century manor house with wide-ranging collection of paintings and furnishings, including Oriental collection. Set in 250 acres of parkland, 1.25 miles from the route. Seasonal opening (0161) 9982331.

Stockport Large industrial suburb that boasts the unusual **Hat Museum** (0161) 3557770. Also **town museum** shows Stockport's history (0161) 4744460. **Art Gallery** has war memorial collection (0161) 4744453. **Floodlit viaduct** dominates much of the town and claims to be Europe's largest brick structure. Underground passages cut into rock underneath the town prior to WWII, and used as war shelters, can now be toured.

INFORMATION FILE

Tourist Information
Warrington: 21 Rylands Street (01925) 442180
Altrincham: 20 Stamford New Road (0161) 9125931
Stockport: Greylaw House, Chestergate (0161) 4744444
Hospitals Altrincham General, Market Street (0161) 9286111. Minor injuries. More major injuries should go to Wythenshawe.
Wythenshawe Hospital, Southmoor Road (0161) 9987070.
Stepping Hill Hospital, Poplar Avenue, Stepping Hill, Stockport (0161) 4831010.
Banks High street banks in Lymm, Stockton Heath, Altrincham, Sale and Stockport.
◶ **D&M Cycles**, 2-4 Hood Lane, Sankey Bridges, Warrington (01925) 653606.
Bikes of Lymm directly on the trail heading east out of Lymm (01925) 753424. Mountain Bike Hire. £12 full day. £9.50 half day.
Lebrams, 197 Manchester Road, Broadheath, Altrincham (0161) 9286600.
Devereux Cycles, 45 Green Lane, Ashton on Mersey, Sale (0161) 9735234.
A1 Cycle Centre, 414-416 Palatine Road, Northenden (0161) 9982882.
Thorpes, 11-13 Wellington Road South, Stockport (0161) 4803992.
Bardseys Cycles, 482 Manchester Road, Stockport (0161) 4324936. Specialists in wheel building and repair services but also general sales and repairs.

Market cross and stocks on rock outcrop, Lymm (section 2)

Viaduct carrying disused railway over Manchester Ship Canal, near Grappenhall
(section 2)

3 STOCKPORT - PENISTONE

Section Distance 29 miles / 47km

The Route The Apethorn-Godley railpath runs to the south of Hyde, whilst walkers have the option of ascending over the lovely Werneth Low Country Park, with great views over Tameside and the west of the Peak District. A mixture of cycle lane, road, track and footpath options, broadly following the Tame Valley, lead to Hadfield and the railpath known as the Longdendale Trail. At the end of the Longdendale Trail, near Woodhead Tunnel, a short, steep climb leads to rougher bridleway over some fine Dark Peak moorland landscape between Langsett Moors and Longside Moss and on to Salters Brook. After a steep road descent to Dunford Bridge the easy, flat Upper Don Trail leads through rolling, green countryside to the market town of Penistone. All in all, this is a remarkably easy crossing of a significant range of upland moors. Even so, you should be aware that ' the tops' of the Dark Peak area can disappear into thick rolling mist, wind or rain at any time of the year even though the weather in the valley below may be fine and still. More often than not there will be a fresh wind on the moors and the temperature will feel a few degrees cooler than down below. Near Salters Brook you are at the highest point on the whole TPT at around 400 metres (1312 feet).

HOTELS & GUESTHOUSES

Needhams Farm, Uplands Road, Werneth Low, Gee Cross, Hyde SK14 3AQ. (0161) 3684610 Fax (0161) 3679106 ▣ charlotte@needhamsfarm.demon.co.uk / www.needhamsfarm.demon.co.uk £17-20. ♦♦♦ ⇲ 1s4d1t1f ▣ ▣ ▮ ⚲ **Dist.** 0.5 miles from walkers' option and 1.25 miles from multi-user route.

Brentwood Guesthouse, 120 Glossop Road, Charlesworth SK13 5HB (01457) 869001. £20 ♦♦♦♦ ▣ ▯ ▮ ⚲ **Dist.** Near route ⊟

Avondale, 28 Woodhead Road, Glossop SK13 7RH (01457) 853132. From ♦♦♦♦ £20. ▣ ▮ ⚲ **Dist.** 1.25 miles

Bridge End, 1 Manor Park, Glossop SK13 7SQ (01457) 854241. ▣ clark@bridge-end-glossop.fsnet.co.uk £18-25 ♦♦♦ ▣ ▯ ▮ ⚲ ✗ **Dist.** 1.5 miles ⊟

Kings Clough Head Farm, Off Monks Road, Glossop SK13 6JZ (01457) 862668. ▣ patricia@keegan p.freeserve.co.uk £18 ⇲ 2d1s ▣ ▯ ▮ ⚲ **Dist.** 2 miles ⊟

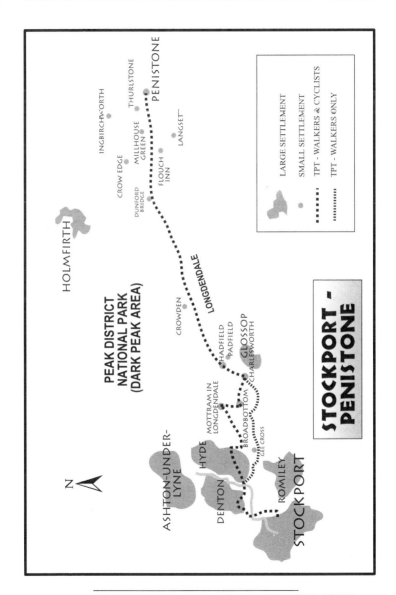

Windy Harbour Farm Hotel, Woodhead Road, Glossop SK13 7QE (01457) 853107. £18. 🛏 4s2d2f 🍽 🍽 ⊡ 🍸 🚲 **Dist.** 1.5 miles. 🚌 Licensed bar, restaurant and tearoom.

The Gables Hotel, 87 Station Road, Hadfield SK13 1AR (01457) 868250. 🖥 welcome@thegableshotel.freeserve.co.uk £20-35. ♦♦♦ 🛏 8s/d 🍽 🍽 🚲 **Dist.** 0.25 miles. Licensed. Close to Hadfield railway station.

Peels Arms, 6 Temple Street, Padfield SK13 1EX (01457) 852719 🖥 Peels@Talk21.com £17.50-25. **R.** 🍽 🍽 ⊡ 🍸 🛠 (bike knowledge) **Dist.** 0.25 miles 🚌

Stanhope Arms, Dunford Bridge S36 6TF (01226) 763104 🖥 stanhope@zoom.co.uk £21 **R** 🛏 3d2t1f singles if required 🍽 🍽 🚲 **Dist.** Next to the trail.

Delmont Grange, Flouch, Hazlehead S36 4HH (01226) 767279 🖥 nancuss@line6ne.net £20 🛏 1d 🍽 🍽 **Dist.** 2 miles (busy A road) 🚌

Millhouse Guest Centre, Carr House Farm, Royd Lane, Millhouse Green, Penistone S36 9NY (01226) 762917. £5-15.00. 🛏 Both B&B and bunkhouse accommodation for groups. 🍽 on request 🍽 🍸 🚲 **Dist.** 1 mile 🚌

Old Crown Inn, Market Street, Penistone S36 6BZ (01226) 7624222. £20 up. **R.** 🛏 4s1d1t 🍽 🍽 ⊡ 🍸 🚲 **Dist.** 0.25 miles

Old Vicarage Guest House, Shrewsbury Road, Penistone S36 6DZ (01226) 370607 🖥 enquiries@old-vicarage.co.uk / www.old-vicarage.co.uk £25 up. **R** 🍽 (lunches only in attached teashop) 🍽 ⊡ 🍸 🚲 **Dist.** Only about 50m off the trail

View over Hyde from walkers' option at Werneth Low Country Park (section 3)

HOSTELS & CAMPSITES

Lymefield Farm Caravan & Camping Site, Broadbottom, Hyde SK14 6AG (01457) 764094. £5 per tent. **Dist.** Just off the route in Broadbottom, down track to Lymefield visitor centre. Same ownership as nearby nursery with tearoom.

Crowden Camping and Caravanning Club Site, Crowden nr Hadfield SK14 7HZ (01457) 866057. From £6.60 per couple. Open End of March-November. 45 pitches. Hot showers and toilets. 5 miles to shops in Hadfield so stock up on food. **Dist.** 0.75 miles.

Crowden Youth Hostel, Crowden-in-Longdendale, Glossop SK13 1HZ (01457) 852135. £8.60 🔁 50 beds - 2 to 12 bedded rooms. 🍽 🍽 🍸 🚲 Seasonal opening: start of April to end of Oct. Self-catering also available. Small shop.YHA membership required. **Dist.** 0.25 miles. Note nearest village services are 5 miles away in Hadfield.

Hazlehead Activity Centre, Hazlehead, Crow Edge, Sheffield S36 4HJ Tel/fax (01226) 370275 / 07931 304268 📧 dominic@hazlehead.co.uk / www.hazlehead.co.uk £8.80-11.75. **R** 🔁 6&9 bed dormitories 🍽 🍽 • 🍸 🚲 ✕ **Dist.** 500m. 🚐 Camping also available.

Langsett Youth Hostel, Langsett, Stocksbridge S36 4GY (01226) 761548. YHA membership required. For group bookings in advance call (01629) 825893. £8.50. 🔁 27 beds in 4,5 and 6 bed dormitories. 🍸 🚲 **Dist.** 1.25 miles south of trail, along busy, fast A616 . Official YHA hostel with basic facilities. There is a cafe in the Langsett village and **Waggon and Horses** pub serves food.

Also camping at **Windy Harbour Farm Hotel**. Call for details - see opposite.

Bridleway section above Longdendale Trail (section 3)

FOOD & DRINK

Reddish Vale Cafe and toilets at visitor centre. See attractions section below for more details.

Mottram in Longdendale has a reasonable selection of pubs and cafes just off the route.

Lymefield Visitor Centre Toilets available in visitor centre itself and cafe inside adjacent nursery. Visitor centre (01457) 765780.

Hadfield main street has a selection of cafes and pubs.

Peel Arms Pub in Padfield does food (01457) 852719.

Stanhope Arms, Dunford Bridge (01226) 763104. Lunches and evening meals except Mondays. 12-2 & 7-9. 12-8 Sundays.

Penistone has a smattering of cafes, pubs and restaurants.

ATTRACTIONS

Reddish Vale Country Park Local nature reserve and centre of a well developed network of bridleways and tracks (0161) 4775637.

Melandra Roman Fort Scheduled ancient monument near the trail between Gamesley and Hadfield. Accessible on foot from the TPT.

Glossop Appearance as dour cotton town hides pretty 17th century conservation area. All large town services about 1.5 miles off TPT. **Heritage Centre** in town centre (01457) 869176.

Longdendale Valley houses the Longdendale Trail, part of the TPT, and a string of impressive reservoirs. Located in ' Dark Peak' area of Peak National Park just north of the forbidding peaty mass of Bleaklow. Navvies who worked on this former railway line are buried in Woodhead Chapel.

Penistone Pennine market town. 13th century church and 18th century Cloth Hall and Shambles.

INFORMATION FILE

Tourist Information
Glossop: The Gatehouse, Victoria Street (01457) 855920

Hospitals No major hospitals on this section across the Pennines.

Banks Main high street banks in Glossop. HSBC with cashpoint in Penistone.

Bike Parking 4 enclosed metal bike lockers at Penistone train station (own lock needed).

🚲 **High Peak Cycles** on main A57 through Glossop (01457) 862427

KG Bikes, 18 Norfolk Street, Glossop (01457) 862427

Lex's Cycles, 112 Sheffield Road, Penistone (01226) 763763

Cyclists at Bullhouse Bridge, Upper Don Trail (section 3)

Cafe in Hadfield, named after the BBC's *League of Gentlemen* comedy (section 3)

4 PENISTONE - BENTLEY

Section Distance 29 miles / 47km

The Route At Oxspring you have a choice of two TPT routes. The main, more direct, option leaves the Upper Don railway path at Oxspring, linking via track, road and footpath to another railway path, the Dove Valley Trail.

Alternatively, you can stay on the railway path at Oxspring, heading south, following the Upper Don and Timberland Trails and the Elsecar Greenway using a variety of surfaces on lanes and bridleways to rejoin the main line of the TPT just east of Wombwell (this option also leads to the Chesterfield Spur - see chapter 5 for details). This alternative passes through the interesting villages of Wortley and Elsecar.

On this section the bleaker foothills of the Pennines around Penistone turn to rolling green countryside. Passing through the regenerated former Wath / Manvers coalfield area your surroundings become increasingly scenic, culminating at the lovely Don Gorge section between Conisbrough and Bentley. Scars on the landscape left by coal mining's decline still remain, but regeneration has gone a long way to making this an attractive countryside area.

HOTELS & GUESTHOUSES

Beckside Cottage, 84 High Street, Silkstone S75 4LR (01226) 792024 DELitsch@btinternet.com £18-32. **R.** 2d **Dist.** 1.25 miles.

Wortley Hall, Wortley S35 7DB (0114) 2882100 Fax (0114) 2830695 wortley.hall@virgin.net £18 and up ♦♦ 5s8d33t8f3tr 18th century listed building in 26 acres of gardens. **Dist.** Near route. Restaurant.

Wortley Guesthouse, Park Avenue, Wortley S35 7DB (0114) 2882179 £23.50 1s1d1f **Dist.** Near route.

20 Kingwell Road, Worsbrough Bridge, Barnsley S70 4HF (01226) 321242. £15. **R** 2d1s1t **Dist.** 0.5 miles. Self-catering facilities.

Button Mill Inn, Park Road, Worsbrough S70 5LJ (01226) 282639. £25. 2s1d3t1f **Dist.** within 0.5 miles.

Wigfield Guest House, 12 Haverlands Lane, Worsbrough Bridge S70 5NQ (01226) 206363 £14 1s2d1t **Dist.** Next to trail.

Grasmere, 12 Waterfield Place, Stairfoot, Barnsley S70 3PZ (01226) 289070 2t **Dist.** 0.5 miles Cutlery provided for take-away food.

Keel Inn Hotel, Canal Street, Barnsley S71 1LJ (01226) 289813 £15 8 rooms **Dist.** 2 miles

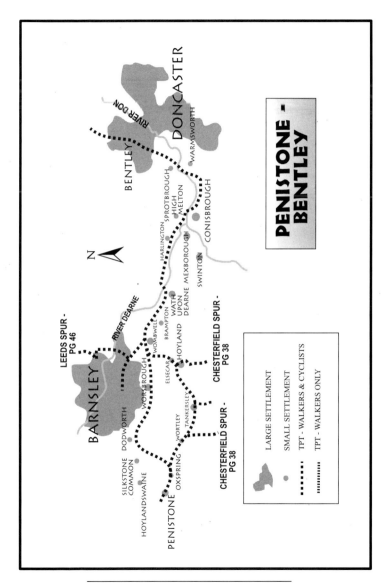

April Cottage, Market Place, Elsecar S74 8HH (01226) 745225
▣ witchespell@folkart.freeserve.co.uk £18 ⤴1d (takes 2 adults plus child)
🍽 🍽 on request ♈ ⊡ (charge) 🚲 **Dist.** Near trail.

Cosy Terrace Cottage, 4 Trent Terrace, Low Road, Conisbrough DN12 3DN
(contact address - 8 Denaby Lane, Old Denaby, Doncaster DN12 4LA)
(01709) 580612 / (01709) 585149 ▣ www.cosycottage.org.uk £50 per night
- whole cottage. ⤴ Sleeps 6-7 people. ⊡ ♈ 🚲 ✗ **Dist.** 0.25 miles 🚌

Harwoods Guest House, 10 Christ Church Road, Doncaster DN1 2QJ (01302)
342244. From £15 ⤴ 1s2d3t2f 🚲 **Dist.** 1.5 miles

Bay Horse Hotel, Cooke Street, Bentley DN5 0DE (01302) 874414. £17
⤴ 1s1d2t2f 🚲 **Dist.** 0.5 miles

There is also a **Travelodge** at **Tankersley Manor** (01226) 350035

HOSTELS & CAMPSITES

Jephroyd Hill Farm, Roper House Lane, Romticle, Thurgoland, Sheffield S35
7BL (0114) 2881709. Tents and touring caravans. Small fee. Toilets and showers,
from spring 2001. Cycle hire and shop planned in future. Open all year, weather
dependent. **Dist.** Next to trail with easy access. Pubs at Thurgoland, 0.25 miles.

Woodland View Caravan Park, 322 Barnsley Road, Hoylandswaine S36 7HA
(01226) 761906. £3-4 per unit. Open April-November. **Dist.** 2 miles

Greensprings Touring Park, Rockley Abbey Farm, Rockley Lane, Worsbrough,
Barnsley S75 3DS (01226) 288298
▣ www.ukparks.co.uk/greensprings £4 per tent. Open April-October.
Dist. 2 miles. Cycle hire can be arranged.

FOOD & DRINK

After Penistone opportunites for food and drink thin out considerably.
The **Potting Shed Cafe** is on Pot House Lane in Silkstone, 1 mile from the TPT.
Wortley Arms Next to TPT in Wortley village centre. Bar snacks and full
meals (0114) 2882245. The **local cafe** is just round the corner.
Harlington Inn, Harlington. Attractive pub, just off the trail, serving food
(01709) 892300.
Pastures Lodge, Dearne Bridge, Mexborough. Carvery restaurant (01709) 579599.
Conisbrough Castle Cafe Outside paygate (01709) 863329.
The **Earth Centre** has a cafe but you must pay the entry fee to get access. See
Attractions section for details.
Boat Inn Attractive location next to TPT on Don Gorge section approaching
Sprotborough. Choice of bar meals and restaurant. 12-2 & 6-9.30 weekdays.
Weekends lunchtime only plus restaurant only on Saturday nights (01302) 857188.
There is a cafe at **Cusworth Hall Country Park**. See Attractions section for details.
Barnsley town centre (on a 3 mile spur from the main route) and Doncaster
town centre (1.5 miles from the main route) have a wide selection of eateries.

Useful information from TPT trail boards (section 4)

Conisbrough viaduct at the western end of the Don Gorge section (section 4)

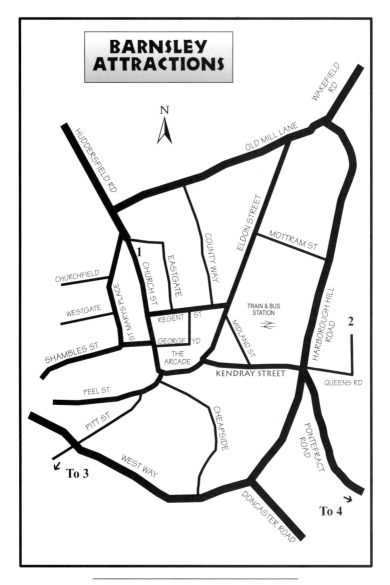

BARNSLEY ATTRACTIONS

FOR ACCOMMODATION SYMBOLS KEY SEE INSIDE COVER

ATTRACTIONS

Silkstone Huskar Pit memorial in churchyard commemorating death of 26 children in mining accident. 1 mile north of TPT at western end of Dove Valley Trail.
Worsbrough Mill in Worsbrough Country Park has demonstrations of stoneground flour-making in the water-powered mill. Parts of the building are centuries old. (01226) 774527. **Rockley Engine House** 17th century blast furnace is nearby.

Barnsley Once a coal mining town that has suffered much due to virtual total pit closure in the area. Local council originated the idea of the Trans Pennine Trail. Large food hall in market (closed Thursdays & Sundays). Attractions (numbered on map) include:
1. Cooper Gallery, Church St. Permanent and visiting exhibitions. Due to reopen in 2001 after renovation works (01226) 242905.
2. Metrodome Leisure Complex, Queens Road. Theme based water rides ideal for kids. (01226) 730060.
3. Locke Park 46 acre park south-west of town centre. Statue of railway builder Joseph Locke and Italianate viewing tower in his wife's memory.
4. Monk Bretton Priory near the start of the Leeds spur, about two miles east of Barnsley town centre. Substantial remains include parts of refectory, gatehouse and 12th century church. English Heritage property - free entry (01226) 204089.

Old Moor Wetland Centre Directly on trail near Wombwell. 250 acres of water, marsh and reedbed, ideal for bird watching. Admission charge. Snack bar & toilets. (01226) 751593.
Coal mining was once a huge employer along much of the Dearne Valley but few signs of it remain. The country park, which the TPT runs through before Bolton Upon Dearne, has an interesting feature at its centre which locates former pits in the area and gives a brief industrial history.
Earth Centre, Conisbrough. TPT passes through grounds of this environmental centre and major lottery project. Admission charge (01709) 322085.
Conisbrough Castle dates from the 12th century and has a spectacular keep. Visible from TPT near Earth Centre. English Heritage - admission charge to non-members (01709) 863329.
Cusworth Hall Country Park 0.75 miles from the TPT, featuring Museum of Local Life in mansion house plus superb landscaped grounds. Free entry (01302) 782342.

Southern Loop Option Attractions
Wortley Pretty, central square with post office/shop, church, tearooms and pub. Impressive Wortley Hall does B&B - see Hotels & Guesthouses section.
Elsecar Lovely valley location plus fine conservation area. Once a model village for local colliery workers. **Elsecar Heritage Centre** Directly on the TPT. Former estate workshops housing Newcomen Beam Engine, Bottle Museum and Hot Metal Press. Working steam railway. (01226) 740203. Toilets.

Doncaster City centre 1.25 miles off main route. Despite much modern development the centre boasts some fine older buildings. Numbers refer to map opposite.

1. Mansion House, High Street. The only one outside of York and London. Open only to groups, by appointment.

2. St Georges Parish Church, Church Way. Rebuilt by Giles Gilbert Scott in mid-nineteenth century in grand neo-gothic style.

3. Corn Exchange and Market Area Includes wide-ranging food market. Tuesday, Thursday, Friday, Saturday (01302) 349631.

4. Doncaster Museum & Art Gallery, Chequer Road. Displays on archaeology, natural history, geology, local history and fine art. Adjacent is the Kings Own Yorkshire Light Infantry Museum. Free admission (01302) 734293.

INFORMATION FILE

Tourist Information
Barnsley: Eldon Street (01226) 206757
Doncaster: Central Library, Waterdale (01302) 734309.
Hospitals Barnsley District General, Gawber Road (01226) 730000.
Doncaster Royal Infirmary, Armthorpe Road (01302) 366666.
Banks All major high street banks in Barnsley and Doncaster town centres.
Barnsley Cycle Centre, 16 Doncaster Road, Barnsley (01226) 287770
Cycosport, 3 Pontefract Road, Barnsley (01226) 204020
Race Scene, 27 Dodworth Road, Barnsley (01226) 215020
Allens Cycles, 23 Barnsley Road, Wombwell (01226) 756281
The Cycle Rack, 4 Church Street, Wombwell (01226) 758810
Don Valley Cycles, 10 Chequer Road, Doncaster (01302) 769531
Doncaster Cycle Centre, 47 Cleveland Street, Doncaster (01302) 360268
Ride a Bike, Ogden Road, Doncaster (01302) 322239

The attractive Boat Inn next to the trail, near Sprotbrough (section 4)

FOR ACCOMMODATION SYMBOLS KEY SEE INSIDE COVER

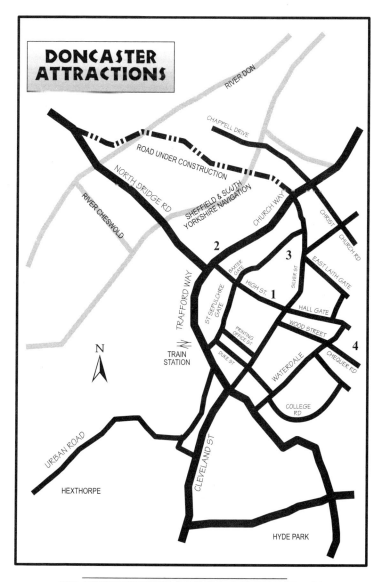

DONCASTER ATTRACTIONS

RIVER DON

CHAPPELL DRIVE

ROAD UNDER CONSTRUCTION

NORTH BRIDGE RD

RIVER CHESWOLD

SHEFFIELD & SOUTH YORKSHIRE NAVIGATION

CHURCH WAY

CHRIST CHURCH RD

2

3

EAST LAITH GATE

BAXTER GATE

SILVER ST

HIGH ST.

1

TRAFFORD WAY

ST SEPULCHRE GATE

HALL GATE

WOOD STREET

4

CHEQUER RD

PRINTING OFFICE ST

N

TRAIN STATION

DUKE ST

WATERDALE

COLLEGE RD

URBAN ROAD

CLEVELAND ST

HEXTHORPE

HYDE PARK

5 BARNSLEY - CHESTERFIELD

Section Distance 35 miles / 55km from Barnsley town centre to Chesterfield town centre using the Wentworth / Beighton option. This is the most complex section in terms of route options, with several route choices heading off the west-east section of the TPT south of Barnsley. There are also spurs to Sheffield and Rotherham centres. Actual distance will, of course, vary depending on your chosen route.

The Route At Oxspring the TPT splits. The southern loop via Wortley, Tankersley and Elsecar rejoins the main line of the TPT just outside Wombwell, but before this you have several opportunities to head off onto the Chesterfield spur. The first comes at Wortley and the second at Tankersley. Both options lead through pretty, rolling green countryside and the large area of woodland north of Grenoside. From here the route picks its way through the suburbs of Chapeltown and Parsons Cross before slotting alongside the River Don at the massive, gleaming Meadowhall shopping complex (a disused railway line is being developed as a more direct alternative along this section). A smaller spur leads off the main route alongside the interesting Five Weirs Walk, towards Sheffield, ending just outside the centre, near the market area. The main route continues south and is nearly all off-road, finally making an impressive entrance to Chesterfield along the lovely Chesterfield Canal.

HOTELS & GUESTHOUSES

Rockingham Arms, 8 Main Street, Wentworth S62 7TL (01226) 742075
From £16.50 **R** ⏍3s4d5t **Dist.** Very near the most easterly link route from the trail south of Barnsley, down to Sheffield. Wide choice of pub meals also available.

Middleton Green Farm, Cinder Hill Lane, Grenoside, Sheffield S35 8NH
(0114) 2453279 ▪ kev@gomoon.demon.co.uk £25-30. **R** ⏍ 3s1d2t 🍽
🔲 🍴 ⚲ ✗ **Dist.** within 0.25 miles NCN route 6. Sauna & jacuzzi. Near pub.

Travel Inn, Attercliffe Common Road, Sheffield S9 2LU (0114) 2422802
£40.95 for all rooms which can accommodate 2 adults and 2 children. 🍽
⚲ **Dist.** Next to Five Weirs Walk spur into Sheffield city centre.

Swan Hotel, 756 Attercliffe Road, Sheffield S9 3RQ (0114) 2447978
▪ swansheffield@btinternet.com / www.swansheffield.co.uk £19.50 **R**
⏍1s8d2t2f 🍽 ⚲ **Dist.** Near both cyclists' and walkers' spur options about halfway along the spur option into Sheffield city centre.

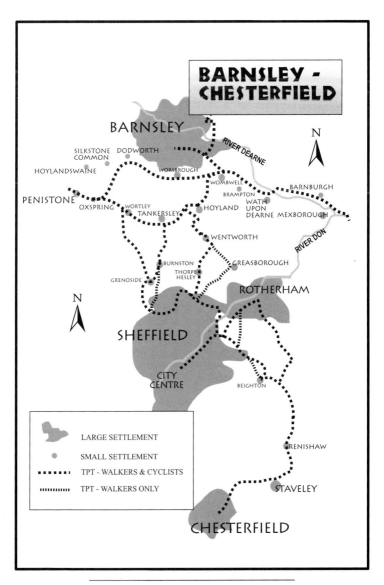

BARNSLEY - CHESTERFIELD

BARNSLEY

RIVER DEARNE

SILKSTONE COMMON

DODWORTH

HOYLANDSWAINE

WORSBROUGH

WOMBWELL

BRAMPTON

BARNBURGH

PENISTONE

OXSPRING

WORTLEY

TANKERSLEY

HOYLAND

WATH UPON DEARNE MEXBOROUGH

WENTWORTH

RIVER DON

BURNSTON

THORPE HESLEY

GREASBOROUGH

GRENOSIDE

ROTHERHAM

SHEFFIELD

CITY CENTRE

BEIGHTON

LARGE SETTLEMENT

SMALL SETTLEMENT

TPT - WALKERS & CYCLISTS

TPT - WALKERS ONLY

RENISHAW

STAVELEY

CHESTERFIELD

N

N

The Rutland Arms, 86 Brown Street, Sheffield S1 2BS (0114) 2729003
Fax: (0114) 2731425 ▆ www.rutlandarms-sheffield.co.uk £18.50-26. **R**. ⦿
⦿ (outdoor yard) **Dist.** 0.5 miles from TPT Sheffield spur end. 0.25 miles
south of city centre. Bar meals available.

Riverside Court Hotel, 4 Nursery Street, Sheffield S3 8GG (0114) 2731962
£19.50 **R** ⦿ ⦿ **Dist.** 0.25 miles to the north west of the TPT end in Sheffield.

Phoenix Hotel, 1 College Road, Rotherham S60 1EY (01709) 364611 £10 **R**
⦿ **Dist.** 0.25 miles. Town centre location, near railway station.

Netherleigh Guesthouse, 7 Gerard Road, Moorgate, Rotherham S60 2PN
(01709) 382753 £11 **R** **Dist.** 0.5 miles. Microwave ovens in twin rooms.

Beighton B&B, 50 High Street, Beighton S20 1EA (0114) 2692004 £14 **R**
⦿ 2s1t ⦿ **Dist.** 0.25 miles west of trail at northern end of Rother Valley
Country Park.

Foresters Arms, Market Street, Staveley S43 3UT (01246) 477455
▆ john.amer@virgin.net £20 **R** ⦿ 1d4t ⦿ ⦿ **Dist.** 0.25 miles. Also
a pub with full restaurant menu.

Sitwell Arms, 39 Station Road, Renishaw S21 3WF (01246) 435226 £23.75
★★★ ⦿ 8s7d ⦿ **Dist.** Near trail.

Anis Louise Guesthouse, 34 Clarence Rd, Chesterfield S40 1LN
(01246) 235412 ▆ neil@anislouise.co.uk / www.anislouise.co.uk £18-20
⦿ 1s2d2t **Dist.** 0.5 miles. Near town centre.

Shakespeare Villa, 3 St. Margarets Drive, Saltergate, Chesterfield S40 4SY
(01246) 200704. £18 ◆◆◆ ⦿ 8s2d ⦿ ⦿ ✗ **Dist.** 0.5 miles

Sheffield and Chesterfield have several major luxury hotels and there are quite a
number of B&Bs outside of Chesterfield town centre. Enquire at local information
offices for details. There are several hotels in Rotheram on Moorgate Road, just
to the south of the centre.

There are no **hostels or campsites** in the immediate vicinity of the TPT on this
stretch. Those prepared to travel several miles off the trail can get details of
campsites from the relevant tourist information offices. For example there is
one at Thrybergh Park, north-east of Rotherham and a number several miles
south and west of Sheffield.

Mock Tudor architecture on Knifesmithgate, Chesterfield (section 5)

FOOD & DRINK

Tankersley Manor Pub, Tankersley. Food available (01226) 744700. Next to the route just north of Westwood Country Park.
Wentworth has two pubs serving food and an upmarket bistro.
The Acorn, Burn Cross. Lunches and dinners, from meals to bar snacks (0114) 2455009. On the route just to the south-west of Chapeltown.
Plenty of pubs in **Grenoside village**, including **Old Harrow Inn** (snacks and lunches 12-2) (0114) 2399907 and the **Old Red Lion** (food 12-2.30 and 6-8.30, Sundays 12-2.30 only) (0114) 2467383. Village shop / post office.
There are plenty of 'chain' food outlets in the **Meadowhall Shopping Complex**, where the route splits for Sheffield city centre or carries on to Rotherham or Chesterfield.
Wentworth House, on the Five Weirs Walk section into Sheffield, has food and Wards beers (0114) 2441594 .
At **Concord Park** the sports centre cafe and golf course club house bar do food and are open to those not using the facilities. See Attractions for details.
Sheffield naturally has plenty of places to eat and drink. One of the more unusual is the **Old Queens Head** on Pond Hill (0114) 2798383. Now a pub it was once a baronial hunting lodge and is the oldest domestic building in Sheffield. Food 11-7 and 12-7 Sundays. The **Fat Cat** and **Kelham Island Brewery** are on Alma Street, north of the centre, near Kelham Island Museum. Real ales and home cooked food. Brewery trips need advance notice (0114) 2494804.
Ulley Country Park, south of Rotheram has toilets and snack machines. (01709) 365332.
In the village of **Ulley** the **Royal Oak** has food lunchtimes and evenings (0114) 2872464
The Mill, on the TPT Chesterfield Canal section 2 miles before Chesterfield, has bar meals and full Sunday lunches (01246) 273807 .
Tapton Lock Visitor Centre, on the Chesterfield canal, has refreshments, information and toilets. Seasonal opening. Phone (01246) 551035 for details.

ATTRACTIONS

Wentworth Attractive village with lots of Victorian architecture located next to the Wentworth estate. 600 feet long frontage of Wentworth Woodhouse stately home (private but walkers' option goes through the grounds).

Thorpe Hesley Once an isolated rural community nicknamed Mutton Town. The Wesley Steps mark the spot where John and Charles Wesley once preached.

Cruck Barn / Concord Park Visitor Centre Toilets including disabled facility: for details of opening ring 0114 2403578. Cafe and toilets approx 150 yards off trail at sports centre and at golf club house (open to public).

Magna UKs first Science Adventure Centre set within vast former Templeborough Steelworks. Have the chance to take control of a JCB digger, feel what it is like to fly or experience the fire tornado. Opens Summer 2001. Next to Meadowhall on the Rotherham spur of the TPT (01709) 720002. www.magnatrust.org

For **Sheffield** attractions see pages 44-45.

Rotherham Another South Yorkshire town based on coal and steel industries. Magnificent **15th century parish church** at heart of town. **Chapel of Our Lady** on Rotherham Bridge is one of three bridge chapels in the whole country. The **Clifton Museum** in Clifton Park houses locally made but world-renowned Rockingham porcelain (01709) 823635. **Boston Castle** 18th century folly perched high above the Rother Valley.

Shirebrook Valley Visitor Centre On southern spur out of Sheffield. Within Local Nature Reserve: ponds, meadow, woodland, pleasant picnic spot. Facilities include local history, wildlife displays, bird hide and toilet (suitable for disabled). Open Spring-Autumn, select days only. Phone (0114) 2735030.

Rother Valley Country Park 750 acres of woods and parkland created from old mineworkings. Bike hire, watersports, golf and fishing available. Visitor centre, toilets (suitable for disabled users) and cafe serving snacks and drinks. Full bar meals available at golf bar near main road entrance (0114) 2471452.

Renishaw Hall and Park Heart of the Sitwell estate with museum, gardens and cafe (01246) 432310. Seasonal opening April-September. Main entrance approx. 1.5 miles from TPT at Renishaw, via A6135 and B6419.

Chesterfield Canal Used for the last stretch of the TPT between Staveley and Chesterfield. Now a pleasant green corridor for walkers and cyclists, it once carried coal and other regional exports from north-east Derbyshire towards the Humber Estuary.

Chesterfield centre is dominated by the bizarrely twisted spire of **St Mary and All Saints Church**, due to unseasoned timber. Monuments to the Foljambe family inside. The **Market Square** is a grand open space with outdoor markets Mondays, Fridays and Saturdays. The city's **Museum and Art Gallery** has exhibits ranging from Roman coins to the windlass used to construct the famous crooked spire - free admission (01246) 345727. Interesting mock Tudor buildings on Knifesmithgate from 1930s.

Chesterfield Canal towpath approaching Tapton Lock (section 5)

INFORMATION FILE

Tourist Information
Sheffield: Surrey Street (0114) 2211900
Accommodation line (0114) 2011011
www.sheffieldcity.co.uk
Rotherham: Central Library, Walker Place (01709) 835904
Chesterfield: Peacock Information Centre, Low Pavement (01246) 345777
Hospital Northern General Hospital, Herries Road, Sheffield (0114) 2434343
Rotherham District General, Moorgate, Rotherham (01709) 820000
Chesterfield & North Derbs Royal, Calow nr Chesterfield (01246) 277271
Banks Several banks in Meadowhall shopping centre, next to route. All major high street banks in Sheffield centre around the junction of Fargate precinct area and High Street. All major banks in Rotherham centre. Staveley has a Lloyds and a Natwest, both with cashpoints. In Chesterfield all major banks with cashpoints are on Market Place and Knifesmithgate.
Transport Bike Bus - service 51 - connects Sheffield and Rother Valley Country Park.
⚅ **Sheffield Cycle Centre**, 832 Barnsley Road, Sheffield Lane Top, Sheffield (0114) 2570650
O Zone Cycles, 143-147 Fitzwilliam Street, Sheffield (0114) 2752233
Birley Cycle Centre, 52 Birley Moor Road, Frecheville, Sheffield (0114) 2648452
Fosters Cycle Centre, Thames Street, Rotherham (01709) 371756
Sondec Cycles, 52 Wellgate, Rotherham (01709) 369607
Killamarsh Cycles, 43 Bridge Street, Killamarsh (0114) 2514600
JE James, Brimington Rd North, Whittington Moor, Chesterfield (01246) 453453

SHEFFIELD ATTRACTIONS

Known as Steel City and also for knife manufacture and silver plate. WWII bombing destroyed much of the old town and the myriad steel mills have shrunk to a handful. Modern redevelopment has included the introduction of a tram system.

1. Sheffield Anglican Cathedral, Church Street. Architecture from the 15th through to the 20th centuries (0114) 2753434.

2. Cutlers Hall This imposing building houses the Cutlers Company's superb collection of silver. Pre-booked parties only (0114) 2728456.

3. City Museum and Mappin Art Gallery Weston Park. From old masters to Victorian works, plus archaeology and social and natural history. Free admission (0114) 2782600. About 1 mile west of the city centre.

4. Town Hall Victorian, grade I listed building. **Peace Gardens** in front of the Town Hall are a fine place to relax in good weather.

5. Graves Art Gallery Above the city library has an outstanding collection of modern art. Free admission (0114) 2782600.

6. Kelham Island Museum, Alma Street. Sheffield's industrial past kept alive; including the mighty River Don steam engine (the most powerful in Europe) and a reconstructed Victorian street with actual self-employed cutlers, grinders and hand forgers. (0114) 2722106.

7. Castle Market Extensive municipal market with a large range of food stalls.

Ruskin Gallery and Craft Centre Modern displays alongside a permanent collection of watercolours, drawings and natural history exhibits. Free admission. New location from 2001 in Town Hall Extension. Enquire at TIC for more details.

The Straddle Warehouse, Sheffield and Tinsley Canal Basin, Sheffield (section 5)

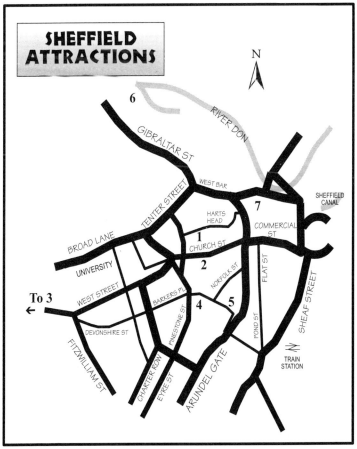

SHEFFIELD ATTRACTIONS

N

6

GIBRALTAR ST

RIVER DON

TENTER STREET

WEST BAR

BROAD LANE

HARTS HEAD

1 CHURCH ST

7

COMMERCIAL ST

SHEFFIELD CANAL

UNIVERSITY

2

NORFOLK ST

FLAT ST

To 3 ←

WEST STREET

BARKERS PL

4

5

DEVONSHIRE ST

PINESTONE ST

POND ST

SHEAF STREET

FITZWILLIAM ST

CHARTER ROW

EYRE ST

ARUNDEL GATE

TRAIN STATION

Tram outside Cutlers' Hall, Sheffield centre (section 5)

6 BARNSLEY - LEEDS

Section Distance 27 miles / 43 km

The Route Although much of the line of this route might be associated with the collapse of traditional industries, most notably coal mining near Barnsley and Wakefield, it passes through some lovely green spaces. Exiting Barnsley on a railway path, you soon join a fine section along the old Barnsley Canal. Following highlights, linked by resurfaced rights of way and canal towpath, include the charming Heath Common and Heath village then the marina at Stanley Ferry on the Aire and Calder Navigation. The canal is used for your final approach into Leeds, arriving at the Royal Armouries Museum. At the time of writing the cycling route finished here, the walking route continuing on to Tetley's Brewery Wharf Museum and the city centre.

HOTELS & GUESTHOUSES

Waterton Park Hotel, Walton Hall, Walton, Wakefield WF2 6PW (01924) 257911 From £55. ★★★ ⟿ 3s42d10t ▐●▌ ▐•▌ ▐ **Dist.** About 300m off the route, next to the Barnsley Canal. Luxury hotel in Georgian mansion on island. Sauna and golf.

Stoneleigh Hotel, 211 Doncaster Road, Wakefield WF1 5HA (01924) 369461. £27.75-30. **R.** ▐●▌ ▐●▌ ▐•▌ ▐ ⑯ **Dist.** 500m down Doncaster Road towards Wakefield.

Bridge Farm Hotel, Wakefield Road, Swillington LS26 8PZ (0113) 2823718. £20-23. ♦♦♦ ⟿ 4s3d3t2f ▐●▌ £10+vat ▐●▌ ▐•▌ ▐ ⑯ **Dist.** 500m

The Griffin at Leeds, 31 Boar Lane, Leeds LS1 5OA (0113) 2422555 From £28 **R** ⟿ 9s21d19tr2f ▐●▌ **Dist.** 0.25 miles. Victorian gothic style building in city centre.

Central Hotel, 35-47 New Briggate, Leeds LS2 8JD (0113) 2941456. From £19 **R** ⟿ 8s8d2t10f ▐●▌ **Dist.** 0.5 miles.

City Centre Hotel, 51 New Briggate, Leeds LS2 8JD (0113) 2429019. From £18.00 **R** ⟿ 3s5d2t3f **Dist.** 0.5 miles.

Boundary Hotel Express, Cardigan Rd, Headingley, Leeds LS6 3AG (0113) 2757700. ▇info@boundaryhotel.co.uk / www.boundaryhotel.co.uk £17.50-25. **R** ⟿ 5s13d ▐●▌ ▐●▌ ▐•▌ ⑯ **Dist.** 2.5 miles. By Headingley stadium. Handy if walking / cycling north from Leeds.

There are also a number of luxury hotels in Leeds near the trail end e.g. Queens Hotel, The Marriott. Contact tourist information by the train station for more details. There are no **campsites** in the immediate vicinity of the trail. **Nostell Priory Holiday Park** is 3.5 miles north-east of the Haw Park section and allows camping. (01924) 863938 for more details. The nearest site to Leeds centre is **Roundhay Caravan & Campsite**, 4 miles to the north-east of the centre (0113) 2652354.

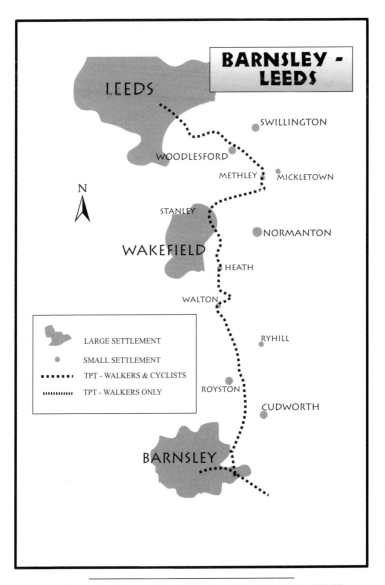

FOOD & DRINK

Squires Tea Room at Waterton Countryside Discovery Centre. Ring (01924) 860282 to check opening hours which vary.

New Inn, Walton. Food available (01924) 255447.

Kings Arms, Heath (01924) 377527. On very scenic section east of Wakefield. Listed building with plenty of nooks, real gas lighting and lovely views over the common. Bar meals and a la carte menu 12-2 and 6-9 daily (all day Sunday). Beer garden. Taylors, Tetleys and Clarks ales.

Plough Inn, Warmfield Lane, Warmfield. About 0.25 miles from the horse riders route. Lunches & dinners (Sunday - lunches only) (01924) 892007.

The Mill House, Stanley, Wakefield. (01924) 290596. Bar / restaurant with family atmosphere. By trail at Stanley Ferry on Aire & Calder Canal. Food 12-9 (9.30 Friday & Saturday).

There are several pubs and fish and chip shops on the road section through **Stanley**.

Rose & Crown, Methley. Food available. (01977) 668235.

Of course, **Leeds** has a huge selection of bars, pubs and restaurants. There is a cafe before the admission till at the **Royal Armouries** (see Leeds attractions, page 50). The Calls area, south-east of the Corn Exchange has more exclusive bars and restaurants, whilst the market has several budget level cafes.

ATTRACTIONS

The Barnsley Canal towpath has been specially renovated for TPT use. Previously the canal, once used to exchange Barnsley coal for supplies from Wakefield, had fallen into neglect. It is now a very pretty section of the route, with reeds and wildlife having colonised much of the waterway. Open countryside alternates with narrow, rocky cuttings.

Waterton Countryside Discovery Centre is at the heart of the Anglers Country Park, an area of woods and lakes east of the Barnsley Canal. Centre 0.75 miles from the route along signed bridleway link. Toilets, cafe, visitor centre and secure cycle parking. For opening details call (01924) 303980.

Walton Hall (see Hotels & Guesthouses section) is the spectacular former home of naturalist Charles Waterton. Many of his strange hybrid taxidermy works and other information are on display at **Wakefield Museum** in the city centre (Wood Street), along with other local history displays (01924) 305351.

Wakefield has its grand **cathedral** at the heart of its pedestrianised shopping centre (01924) 373923 . The **Art Gallery**, Wentworth Terrace, has works by renowned local sculptors Henry Moore and Barbara Hepworth (01924) 305796.

Thwaite Mills, Stourton, Leeds is a former seed crushing and putty mill, now a museum with original water-powered machinery and a steam powered crane. Just off the TPT, on the River Aire, before Knostrop Cut. Admission charge (0113) 2496453.

Look out for **artworks** on the Leeds section of the route.

Hale's History Tree, carved from a dead beech tree.
Found on Church Road, Hale (section 1)

A sunny summer Sunday means a busy TPT section by the A1 bridge over the River Don (section 4)

The TPT uses the picturesque River Don towpath at Sprotbrough Lock (section 4)

Summer flowers on the TPT near the Earth Centre (section 4)

Riding on the TPT in Greno Wood (section 5)

Bridleway section of TPT above
Longdendale Trail (section 3)

Walkers and cyclists along the Aire & Calder canal towpath at Swillington (section 6)

The Kings Arms in an attractive location by the TPT on Heath Common (section 6)

INFORMATION FILE

Tourist Information
Wakefield: Town Hall, Wood Street (01924) 305000
Leeds: Gateway Yorkshire, The Arcade, City Station (0113) 2425242
Hospitals Pinderfields Hospital, Aberford Road, Wakefield (01924) 201688
Leeds General Infirmary, Great George Street, Leeds (0113) 3926886
Banks Major high street banks in Wakefield centre around Wood Street / precinct
area and in Leeds centre around the Trinity Street shopping area.
🚲 **Halfords Superstore**, 78 Ings Road, Wakefield (01924) 387474
Psycles Discount Bikes, 174 Kirkgate, Wakefield (01924) 332213
The Bike Chain, 119-121 Vicar Lane, Leeds (0113) 2465339

LEEDS ATTRACTIONS

Leeds combines a modern shopping centre with some grand Victorian
architecture. Several attractive shopping arcades in the modern centre. Many
former industrial buildings alongside the River Aire have been renovated for
housing or offices.

Numbers refer to map opposite.

1. Dark Arches Bridge lies beneath the vaulted ceiling of the massive railway
station viaduct and has been compared to catacombs. It leads to **Granary
Wharf Craft Arcade**.
2. Tetley's Brewery Wharf Tour of brewery plant and shire horses (0113) 2420666.
3. Thwaite Mills Industrial Museum Alongside TPT before your entry into city
centre. Previously used for a great variety of grinding activities including the
production of oil, dye, corn and putty. Now houses restored water and steam
powered machinery (0113) 2496453.
4. Royal Armouries New home of the national arms and armour collection.
Five themed galleries plus demonstrations of jousting, falconry and
horsemanship. Admission fee (0113) 2201999.
5. Victorian Town Hall with giant columns and 225ft clock tower. The **Art Gallery**,
next door, has a strong collection of paintings from Victorian times onwards.
6. Market Hall Beautiful, complex structure of glass, iron and stone with a
huge choice of food.
7. Corn Exchange Unique roof caps this oval building. Now houses speciality
shops. White Cloth Hall behind Corn Exchange undergoing similar restoration.
8. Armley Mills on Canal Road was once the world's largest woollen mill. Now
a museum housing displays on the history of wool and a museum. Admission
charge (0113) 2637861.

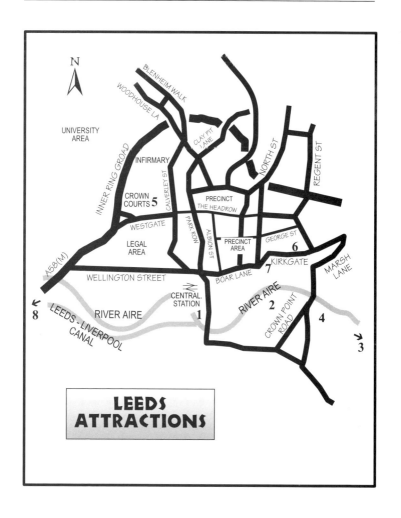

7 BENTLEY - SELBY

Section Distance 29 miles / 47km

The Route Pleasant red brick villages dot the flat agricultural land of South and North Yorkshire as you shadow the River Don, flowing north towards the Ouse. Agriculture's open expanse is broken by numerous huddles of trees, such as Owston Wood before a quiet road link leads onto the dead straight and very peaceful New Junction Canal. All the while the cooling towers of more easterly power stations loom on the horizon. Minor roads and tracks are then used before you follow the Selby Canal into the market town of Selby, whose highlight is the outstanding medieval abbey. This is a relatively quiet and sparsely settled section of the TPT, so it may well pay off to plan where you are staying and book in advance. Although there is a reasonable amount of accommodation in Selby there are much fewer opportunities in the succession of small villages before this. Food and drink opportunities are also limited so try to tie in with opening hours.

HOTELS & GUESTHOUSES

Brewers Arms Hotel, Pontefract Road, Snaith DN14 9JS (01405) 862404 Around £20 7s3d plus extra annex capacity **Dist.** 0.25 miles.

Forresters Arms, Carlton DN14 9LN (01405) 860315. £26-29. **R. Dist.** 0.25 miles.

Chester Court Lodge, Chester Court Lane, Camblesforth YO8 8JD (01757) 618634 Jeanshepard@handbag.com £20. **R.** 1s1d1t on request **Dist.** 0.5 miles Tents also welcome.

Royal Oak Inn, Main Street, Hirst Courtney YO8 8QT (01757) 270633. £30 2s2d5t **Dist.** Next to route. Camping also allowed; call for details.

Hazeldene, 34 Brook Street, Selby YO8 4AR (01757) 704809. www.selbynet.co.uk/hazeldene £22-23 ♦♦ 2s6d **Dist.** 0.5 miles. Bikeshop nearby. Near town centre services.

Londesborough Arms Hotel, Market Place, Selby YO8 0NS (01757) 707355 From £25 **Dist.** 0.25 miles.

The Willows, Cockrett Close, Off White Street, Selby YO8 4BS (01757) 701271 £17-22 **Dist.** 0.5 miles.

Note for campers: There are no dedicated campsites on this section but see above for B&B providers who allow camping.

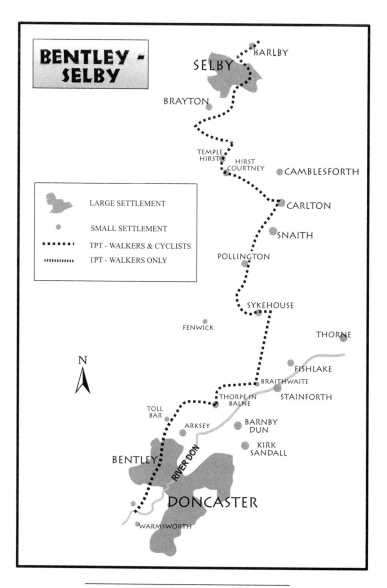

FOOD & DRINK

Plough Inn, Arksey. Attractive village setting 1.25 miles east of TPT. Food available (01302) 872472.
Owston Park Lodge, on A19 west of Owston Wood section, 1.25 miles from the route (01302) 700571. Food all day, ranging from sandwiches to chefs specials. Part of Tom Cobleigh chain.
Hare & Hounds, Fishlake
Sykehouse Old George Inn has restaurant. Closed Mondays (01405) 785635.
Royal Oak Inn at Hirst Courtney does lunches and evening meals (01757) 270633. Plenty of pubs in **Snaith** and lots of eateries in **Selby**, including an Italian bakers at the indoor market.

ATTRACTIONS

Arksey Tiny but delightful village centre with church, almshouses and pub.
Fishlake village was once an inland port. Sign by post office details village history. Green picnic area here was formerly a landing stage for fishermen on the once wide river. Ancient church doorway has extremely rare and fine Norman carving.
Snaith Variety of shops and pubs. Elegant church is the central village landmark.
Carlton Home to Victorian Gothic mansion house, **Carlton Towers**. Once a conventional Jacobean House, it was turned into a mock medieval construction by two young eccentrics in the 1870s. Now a private building that you glimpse from the main road. Occasionally open for weekend events.
Selby Town centre dominated by the superlative **Abbey**, a mix of styles from Norman times onwards. Most impressive feature is the nave, with its rows of Norman arches 'stacked' upon each other. The **Washington Window** is also rightly famous. Next to the Abbey the broad **market place** is joined by Finkle Street, leading to Micklegate, the shopping heart of the town with some fine old buildings. The old **dock and shipyard** area is lined with impressive edifices along Ousegate.

Looking down New Junction Canal (section 7)

INFORMATION FILE

Tourist Information
Park Street, Selby (01757) 703263
A&E Hospital War Memorial Hospital, Doncaster Road, Selby (01757) 702664.
Banks HSBC in Snaith, no cashpoint. Lloyds, Barclays, HSBC, Natwest and
Halifax (Link) all with cashpoints around Market Place, in front of the Selby Abbey.
🚲 **Forward Cycle Store**, on A19 in northern part of Bentley (01302) 874164
Robson Cycles, 78 Owston Road, Carcroft (01302) 722275. 2.25 miles west
of the route at Owston Wood. **A Donoghue**, 8 The Crescent, Selby (01757)
706037 **Selby Bike Centre**, 49 Gowthorpe, Selby (01757) 702385

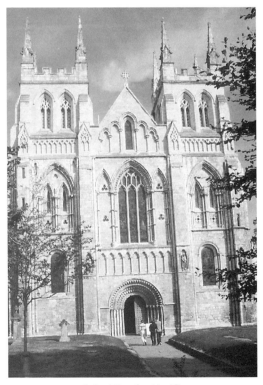

Selby Abbey (section 7)

8 SELBY - YORK

Section Distance 18 miles / 29 km

The Route Flat agricultural land once again makes for easy going. There are a number of small, attractive red-brick villages near the route before the final passage of the TPT through Bishopthorpe and into the outskirts of York. The final approach to the historic core of York is a fine one, passing over the racecourse and alongside the River Ouse at Rowntree Park. After passing along the river and through the centre you finish at the grand train station. Much of the section is on the excellently surfaced York - Selby Railpath, with path and road links at either end.

HOTELS & GUESTHOUSES

Dairyman's Cottage, 14 Kellfield Road, Riccall YO19 6PG (01757) 248532 £18 ⬧ 1s1d1t1f ▣ ⏚ ⬧ (by arrangement) ⬧ **Dist.** 0.25 miles

South Newlands Farm, Selby Road, Riccall YO19 6QR (01757) 248203 £18-22 ♦♦♦ ⬧ 2d1t1f ▣ ⬧ ⏚ ⬧ Basic tools. **Dist.** 0.25 miles

Avondale Guesthouse, 61 Bishopthorpe Road, York YO23 1NX (01904) 633989. £19-22. ♦♦♦ ⬧ **Dist.** 0.25 miles west of the trail at Rowntree Park.

Bowen House, 4 Gladstone Street, Huntingdon Rd, York YO31 8RF Tel/fax (01904) 636881. ▣ valwoodyork@aol.com £18.50-24♦ ♦♦ ⬧6s/d/t/f ⬧ ✗**Dist.** 1 mile. Quiet location north-east of the centre, near the River Foss.

Mont Clare Guest House, 32 Claremont Terrace, Gillygate, York YO31 7EJ (01904) 627054. ▣ MontclareY@aol.com £25. **Dist.** 0.5 miles. Just north of historic minster area.

Riverside Walk, Earlsborough Terrace, Marygate, York YO30 7BQ (01904) 620769 ▣ Julie@riversidewalkbb.demon.co.uk £20-27.50 ♦♦♦ ⬧ ⏚ ⬧ **Dist.** 0.25 miles. North of River Ouse, opposite train station.

Romley House, 2 Millfield Road, York YO23 1NQ (01904) 652822 ▣ www.romleyhouse.co.uk £18-25. **R.** ▣ ⏚ ⬧ **Dist.** 0.25 miles ▤

Saxon House Hotel, 71-73 Fulford Road, York YO10 1BD (01904) 622106 Fax (01904) 633764 ▣ saxon@househotel.freeserve.co.uk / www.saxonhousehotel.co.uk £24-38. **R.** ⬧ ⏚**Dist.** 0.5 miles, on A19, south east of city centre. Residents' bar.

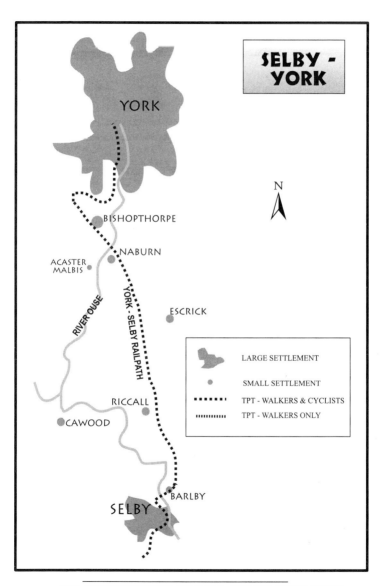

SELBY -
YORK

YORK

N

BISHOPTHORPE

NABURN

ACASTER
MALBIS

ESCRICK

RIVER OUSE

YORK - SELBY RAILPATH

LARGE SETTLEMENT

SMALL SETTLEMENT

TPT - WALKERS & CYCLISTS

TPT - WALKERS ONLY

RICCALL

CAWOOD

BARLBY

SELBY

HOSTELS & CAMPSITES

York International Youth Hostel, Water End, Clifton, York YO30 6LP
(01904) 653147. ■ york@yha.org.uk / www.yha.org.uk £11.25-15.05
⚑ Dormitories & s/t/tr 🍴 🍴 ⬚ 🍸 🚲 Also self-catering, games room,
cyber cafe, book exchange and bird watching. **Dist.** 1.25 miles to north of centre.

York Backpackers Hostel, Micklegate House, 88 Micklegate, York YO1 6JX
(01904)677720 ■ yorkbackpackers@cwcom.net/ www.yorkbackpackers.mcmail.com
£9-15. **R.** ⚑ 135 beds. 🍴 🍴 ⬚ 🍸 🚲 ✗ **Dist.** 0.25 miles. Near centre.
Self-catering facilities, bar & continental cafe, internet access.

York Youth Hotel, 11/13 Bishophill Senior, York YO1 6EF (01904) 625904
■ info@yorkyouthhotel.demon.co.uk £14-15 ⚑ 120 beds 🍴 ⬚ 🍸 🚲
✗ Self-catering facilities, bar and games room. **Dist.** 0.25 miles. 🚌

Naburn Lock Caravan & Camping Park, Naburn YO19 4RU (01904) 728697
14 tent pitches from £8.50. March - November. Shop, laundry and showers.
■ www.scoot.co.uk/naburn_lock_caravan/ **Dist.** 1 mile.

Chestnut Farm Holiday Park, Acaster Malbis YO23 2UQ (01904) 704676
25 tent pitches from £7. April - October. Wide-ranging facilities including shop, laundry
and showers. ■ alison@chestnuthp.freeserve.co.uk **Dist.** approx. 1.5 miles.

Mount Pleasant Holiday Park, Acaster Malbis YO23 2UA (01904) 707078
60 tent pitches from £7. March - 8th January. Shop, laundry, showers.
Dist. approx. 1.5 miles.

Riverside Caravan and Camping Site, Ferry Lane, Bishopthorpe YO2 1SB
(01904) 704442. **Dist.** 0.5 miles.

Rowntree Park Caravan Club Site, Terry Avenue, York (01904) 658997.
Showers, toilets ⬚ 🍸 6 tent pitches **Dist.** Nearby trail on your entry to York
by the River Ouse. Facilities for disabled.

FOOD & DRINK

Riccall Food outlets and pubs.
Naburn Food at the **Blacksmith's Arms** (01904) 623464.
Bishopthorpe Several village pubs.
Tesco supermarket cafe Handily open 24 hours. Just off trail on Tadcaster
Road near college buildings on York outskirts.

York itself has a huge range of eating and drinking places, including some fine
historic pubs.

Crossing the Ouse south of Bishopthorpe (section 8)

ATTRACTIONS

Riccall Quiet and pretty village. Norway's Harold Hardrada stopped here in 1066 on his way to defeat by King Harold at Stamford Bridge.
Naburn Lavish Ouse Navigation Trustees banqueting house just south of village cost £3,000 in 19th century!
Bishopthorpe Grand **Bishop's Palace**. Main buildings date from 15th century and chapel from 13th century.

INFORMATION FILE

Tourist Information De Grey Rooms, Exhibition Sq. (01904) 621756. This organisation also has a branch at the railway concourse. York Tourism Bureau is at 20 George Hudson Street (01904) 620557.
Hospital York District Hospital, Wigginton Road (01904) 631313.
 Banks All major high street banks in York Centre.
 🚲 **Bob Trotter Cycles**, 13-15 Lord Mayors Walk (01904) 622868 **Bike Shack**, 30 Walmgate (01904) 622044 **Cycle Heaven** 2 Bishopthorpe Road (01904) 636578 **York Cycleworks**, 14-16 Lawrence Street (01904) 626664

YORK ATTRACTIONS

York is so crammed full of historical buildings, pubs, interesting streets and byways and museums that it is impossible to do more than cover the highlights. For a comprehensive guide to historical walks and other city features see 'York Walks' by the same author, from Excellent Books.

• **York Minster** (1) The largest Gothic church in northern Europe, built over a 250 year timespan. The Lady Chapel contains the Great East Window, the size of a tennis court and the largest area of medieval glass in the world. Norman Doomstone and William of York's tomb in crypt. From choir screen look up 200 feet into the central tower. Undercroft has Roman remains and you can walk round the massive supports of the central tower. Open daily, except Sunday morning (services only) (01904) 639347.
• The **Treasurer's House** (2) Originally the house of the keeper of the Minster's affairs, it was restored by a 20th century industrialist. April - Oct. Admission charge (01904) 624427. (NT members free). Free entry to tea room / art gallery.
• **Yorkshire Museum** (3) One of the finest collections of archaeology, geology and natural history in the north of England. Open daily (01904) 629745.
• **National Railway Museum** (4) Housed in the old Leeman Road steam depot and a newer building, it includes classics such as Victorian and Edwardian royal carriages and the Mallard. Open daily. Admission charge (01904) 621261.
• **Micklegate Bar** (5) Historically, the most important gateway into the city and famous as the place traitors' heads were exhibited on poles. Houses **Micklegate Bar Museum** telling the story of the **City Walls**. Admission charge.
• **The Shambles** (6) One of the best preserved medieval streets in Europe. Margaret of Clitherow lived at no.39 which is now a shrine to her memory; she was pressed to death with heavy stones for harbouring Jesuits.
• **Merchant Adventurers' Hall** (7) Huge timber-framed building deriving its name from the powerful medieval trading organisation (01904) 654818.
• **Jorvik Viking Centre** (8) Recreation of a tenth century Coppergate Alley. Perhaps the strongest reminder of the Vikings' presence in the city is the 'gate' ending of many street names. Open daily. Admission charge (01904) 643211.
• **Clifford's Tower** (9) The original wooden Norman fortress here was later replaced with stone and was once used as the Royal Mint. Its name comes from Roger Clifford, hung from the tower wrapped in chains in the 14th century. Magnificent views from the upper rim. Open daily. Admission charge (01904) 646940.
• **Castle Museum** (10) England's most popular museum of everyday life. Great visual appeal includes completely reconstructed Jacobean, Georgian, Victorian and 20th century rooms and completely reconstructed Edwardian Street. Open daily (01904) 653611.
• **Barley Hall** (11) Reconstructed townhouse of a medieval York citizen. April-Oct. Admission charge (01904) 610275.

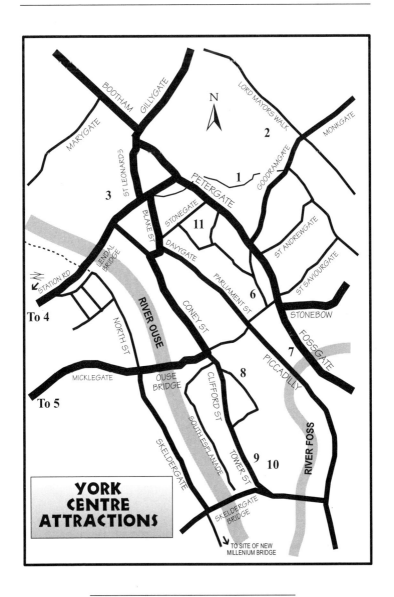

YORK CENTRE ATTRACTIONS

9 SELBY - BROUGH / WELTON

Section Distance   20 miles / 32km

The Route One of the quietest sections on the whole TPT, you follow the slow, wide Ouse through some tiny villages to the base of the Wolds. Population is sparse and Howden, with its highly unusual church, is the only town of any size. Village services become more frequent and wide-ranging as you reach such pretty settlements as Brantingham and Welton at the southern tip of the Yorkshire Wolds. Walkers' and cyclists' routes diverge for considerable distances, walkers more often following the River Ouse's banks. The going is flat, with wide vistas over the river and huge fields.

HOTELS & GUESTHOUSES

Hagthorpe House, Selby Road, Brackenholme near Hemingborough YO8 6EL (01757) 638867 ▧ hagthorpe@supanet.com £16-20. ⟿ 1d1t ⓘ⌾ ⌾ ❦
✗ **Dist.** 2.25 miles east of Hemingborough along the A63. ⛟

Minster View Hotel, 2-3 Corn Market Hill, Howden DN14 7BU (01430) 430447. £16
⟿ 3s5d6t ⓘ⌾ ⓘ⌾ ❦ ⑳ **Dist.** 0.25 miles

Briarcroft Hotel, Clifton Gardens, Goole DN14 6AR (01405) 763024 £20. **R.**
⟿ 5s12d ⓘ⌾ ⓘ⌾ ❦ ⑳ **Dist.** 2.5 miles from walking route, 3.5 miles from cycling route.

Fairways Farm, Northfield Close, South Cave HU15 2EW (01430) 421285. £20.
❦ ⑳ **Dist.** Approx 1.5 miles from cycling route, 2.5 miles from walking route.

Silver Trees, 23 Castle Drive, South Cave HU15 2ES (01430) 423616. £16.
⟿ 1s1d1t ⓘ⌾ ⓘ⌾ ⌾ ❦ ⑳ **Dist.** Approx 1.5 miles from cycling route, 2.5 miles from walking route.

Turks Trod House, 67a Church Street, South Cave HU15 2EP (01430) 423931.
⟿ 2d2t ⓘ⌾ ⌾ ❦ ⑳ Basic tools. **Dist.** Approx 1.5 miles from cycling route, 2.5 miles from walking route.

Littleover Lodge Guest House, Hill Top, Howden Croft Hill, Ellerker HU15 2DE (01430) 421821. £16 ⓘ⌾ ⌾ ❦ ⑳ **Dist.** Approx 1.5 miles from cycling route, 2.5 miles from walking route.

Woldway, 10 Elloughton Rd, Brough HU15 1AE (01482) 667666. £16
⟿ 1s1d1t ⓘ⌾ ⌾ ❦ ⑳ **Dist.** 0.75 miles from walking route, 0.5 miles from cycling route.

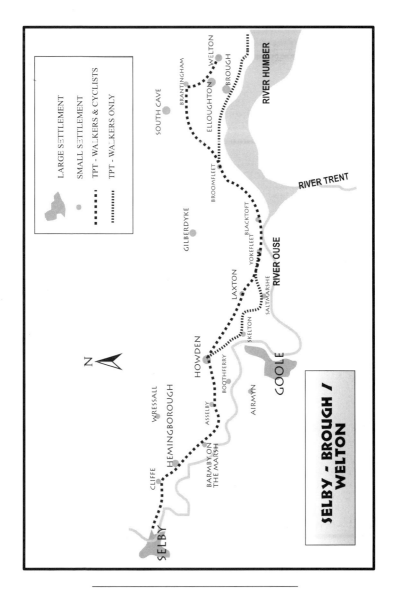

HOSTELS & CAMPSITES

Hope & Anchor Inn, Blacktoft DN14 7YW (01430) 440441. 4 tent pitches. Hot water, toilets and cafe. Next to route.

Waudbys Caravan & Camping Park, Brough Road, South Cave HU15 2DB (01430) 422523. April - January. Showers and shop. 0.25 miles from cycling route.

FOOD & DRINK

Nearly every small village along the route seems to have its own pub:

Laxton **Bricklayers Arms** serves Sunday lunch and evening meals on selected days only. Call in advance to confirm food required (01430) 430111.
Broomfleet **Red Lion** serves drinks only (01430) 422426.
Blacktoft **Hope & Anchor** (01430) 440441.
Ellerker has a shop and pub and the a la carte **Black Horse Restaurant** where 3 courses are around £25 (01430) 423270.
Brantingham **Triton** restaurant (01482) 667261.
Elloughton **Half Moon** (01482) 667362.
Welton's **Green Dragon Hotel** Food served. Dick Turpin, infamous highwayman, captured here in 1739 (01482) 666700.

Time out at Brantingham post office (section 9)

FOR ACCOMMODATION SYMBOLS KEY SEE INSIDE COVER

Weighton Lock where Market Weighton Canal meets the River Humber (section 9)

ATTRACTIONS

190 foot tower of St Marys Church at **Hemingborough**. Pencil-like spire of fine white stone is a landmark for miles around. Inside are fine bench-end carvings. Key from Church House or garage. The main street contains a number of fine 19th century houses.

Howden Small market town dominated by the **Church of St Peter**. The arch of the collapsed 17th century choir remains and dramatically frames the rest of the church. Remains of the ruined chapter house have fine carving. Former **Bishop's Palace** now a private residence but a path to playing fields leads right by it. It was once a stopping place for the medieval Prince Bishops of Durham who controlled vast areas of the locality. Attractive **Market Place** and brick **Market Hall**.

Blacktoft Jetty is important for ships travelling up the Ouse to Goole; it's a handy laying up point to wait at until the tide has risen enough for them to go on. Ships from all countries dock here, especially from the Baltic area.

Brantingham is perhaps the quaintest of all the villages on this section, with its brick terraces decorated with wooden porches. The village pond is backed by estate land. The elaborate war memorial was built from parts of the old Victorian Town Hall in Hull.

Welton Much grand architecture, for example Welton Grange, created by wealthy Hull shipping merchants who treated the village as a country retreat. Church has Pre-Raphaelite windows made by William Morris's craftsmen.

INFORMATION FILE

🚲 **Discount Cycling**, 115 Pasture Road, Goole (01405) 764405
Banks HSBC banks in Howden and South Cave (1 mile from cycling route), both with external cashpoints.

The Bricklayers Arms at Laxton (section 9)

FOR ACCOMMODATION SYMBOLS KEY SEE INSIDE COVER

Stained glass window, village hall, Blacktoft (section 9)

The quiet roads on the cyclists' option, north of the River Humber   (section 9)

10 BROUGH / WELTON - HORNSEA

Section Distance 28 miles / 46 km

The Route The interim cycling option continues through the Wolds whilst the walking route maintains its course along the Humber, passing under the truly spectacular Humber Bridge. Through the grand old port of Hull you head onto the Hornsea Rail Trail, which leads through quiet agricultural countryside to the resort of Hornsea, with its traditional seaside food and entertainments. Accommodation planning may be different for walkers, cyclists and horse riders, as the various user route options are separated by up to 2 miles in some places.

HOTELS AND GUESTHOUSES

B&B@103, 103 Ferriby High Road, North Ferriby HU14 3LA (01482) 633637 / mobile 07808 387651 ▆ simpson.103@usa.net / www.bnb103.co.uk £15 ♦♦♦ ⌐ 1d1s1t ⚅ **Dist.** approx 1 mile. ▩

Country Park Lodge, Cliff Road, Hessle Foreshore, Hessle HU13 0HB (01482) 640652. £24.50 ⌐8 rooms ▥ at adjacent Bridge Suite Restaurant. **Dist.** On walking route, 1.25 miles from cycling route.

Sandford, 79 Ferriby Road, Hessle HU13 0HU (01482) 648655. £18-20. **R**. ⌐ 1s2d2t ▥ ⚅ **Dist.** 0.5 miles. Self-catering facilities.

Acorn Guest House, 719 Beverley High Road, Hull HU6 7JN (01482) 853248. £15-20 ♦♦♦ ⌐ 2s2t2tr ▢ ▌ ⚅ ✗ **Dist.** 1.5 miles.

Admiral Hotel, 234 The Boulevard, Hull HU3 3ED Tel & Fax (01482) 329664. £13.50-17.00. ♦♦ ⌐ 2s1t1f ▥ ▌ ⚅ ✗ **Dist.** Within 0.5 miles of both walking and cycling routes, just over a mile west of Hull centre.

The Arches, 38 Saner Street, Hull HU3 2TR (01482) 211558. £15-25. ♦♦♦ ⌐ 2s2d1t ⚅ **Dist.** Within 0.5 miles of both walking and cycling routes, just over a mile west of Hull centre.

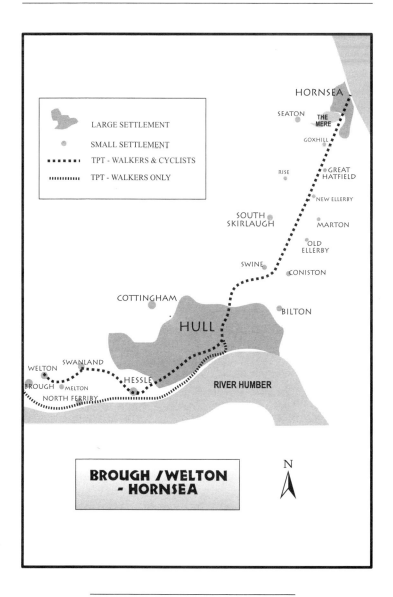

LARGE SETTLEMENT

SMALL SETTLEMENT

TPT - WALKERS & CYCLISTS

TPT - WALKERS ONLY

HORNSEA

SEATON   THE MERE

GOXHILL

RISE   GREAT HATFIELD

NEW ELLERBY

SOUTH SKIRLAUGH   MARTON

OLD ELLERBY

SWINE   CONISTON

COTTINGHAM

BILTON

HULL

WELTON   SWANLAND

BROUGH   MELTON   HESSLE

NORTH FERRIBY   RIVER HUMBER

BROUGH /WELTON - HORNSEA

N

Conway-Roseberry Hotel, 86 Marlborough Avenue, Hull HU5 3JT
(01482) 445256 / 07909 517328. £17-30. **R** ⚲ 2s2d2t ◉ ⛿
Dist. 1 mile from cycling route, 2.25 miles from walking route.

Earlsmere Hotel, 76-78 Sunny Bank, Hull HU13 1LQ (01482) 440150.
💻 su@earlsmerehotel.karoo.co.uk £18-28. ♦♦♦ ⚲ 2t 6d ◉ ⛿ ✕
Dist. 0.5 miles from cycling route, 1.75 miles from walking route. Just to the
north of West Park, west of Hull centre.

England's Rose Holiday Home, 194 Roslyn Road, East Ella, Hull HU3 6XH
(Contact address: 9 Minnies Grove, Walton Street, Hull HU3 6JP) (01482)
352733. £20-31 per house. **R**. ⚲ Sleeps 4. ⸱ ⛿ Self catering.
Dist. 0.75 miles from cycling option, 1.5 miles from walking option.

Quality Royal Hotel, 170 Ferensway, Hull HU1 3UF (01482) 325087.
💻 admin@gb611.u-net.com £67.50. **R** ⚲ 37s37d ◉ ◉ ⸱ ⛟
Dist. Within 0.25 miles. Fully equipped leisure centre.

Trees Guesthouse, 132 Sunny Bank, Hull HU3 1LE (01482) 448822. £16-18.
⚲ 4s4d4t ◉ ◉ ⸱ ⛟ ⛿ **Dist.** 0.5 miles from cycling route, 1.75 miles
from walking route. 🚌

Admiralty Guesthouse & Tearoom, 7 Marine Drive, Hornsea HU18 1NJ
(01964) 536414. £15-19. **R** ⚲ 6s7d ◉ ◉ ⛿ **Dist.** 100 yds from end.

Ashburnam Guest House, 1 Victoria Avenue, Hornsea HU18 1NH
(01964) 535118. £15. **R** ⚲ 1s3d1t2f ⛿ **Dist.** 0.25 miles from route end.

Merlstead Hotel, 59 Eastgate, Hornsea HU18 1NB (01964) 533068. £23.00
♦♦♦ ⚲ 1s1d3t1f ◉ ⛿ **Dist.** 0.25 miles.

Sandhurst Guesthouse, 3 Victoria Avenue, Hornsea HU18 1NH
(01964) 534653 💻 rhodes@hornseals.fsnet.co.uk £15. **R** ⚲ 5s1d
◉ ⛟ ⛿ **Dist.** 0.25 miles from route end.

Westgate Mews, Back Westgate, Hornsea HU18 1BL (01964) 533430
💻 walker@h'sea.freeserve.co.uk £25-37. **R** ⸱ ⛟ ⛿ Self-catering (1 flat
and 1 cottage available). **Dist.** 0.5 miles. Near Hornsea Mere. Prices quoted
are pro-rata and apply also to weekly rates.

HOSTELS & CAMPSITES

Hull International Hostel, 4 Malm Street, Boulevard, Hull HU3 2TF (01482) 216409
£6-10. ⸱ ⛟ ⛿ **Dist.** Within 0.5 miles of both walking and cycling routes,
just over a mile west of Hull centre. Self-catering facilities available.

Burton Constable Caravan & Camping Park, Old Lodge, Sproatley HU11
4LN (01964) 562508. **R** Toilets plus showers.⛟ ⛿ **Dist.** Approx. 3 miles east
of Hornsea Rail Trail, in the lovely grounds of Burton Constable Hall.

Cowden Caravan & Leisure Park, Eelmere Lane, Cowden HU11 4UL
(01964) 527393   £3. **R.** ⌐•⌐ ✗ **Dist.** 3.5 miles south of Hornsea. March1st - Jan 1st. Shop.

FOOD & DRINK

Swan & Cygnet, Swanland, serves food (01482) 634571 / 631877.
Riverside Bar is on the foreshore (walkers' route) at Hessle. A la carte meals and bar snacks. Part of Country Park Lodge accommodation (01482) 640526.
Marquis of Granby Pub, Hessle (on cycling route) (01482) 626251.
The **Railway** public house, nearby the trail at New Ellerby has food (01964) 563770.
If visiting **Burton Constable Hall**, 2.5 miles off the trail, there is a **tea room** just outside the paygate. See Attractions below for more details.
The Wrygarth pub at Great Hatfield, next to trail (01964) 536000.

ATTRACTIONS

Swanland Pretty wolds village with shop and duck pond (cycling route).
The incredible **Humber Bridge** soars above **Hessle**. Walking route passes underneath the bridge but cyclists currently have to make a detour. 533 feet high twin towers and 1542 yard main span hung between them from immensely thick cables. National Cycle Network route number one from Harwich to Hull uses what must be one of the most spectacular cycle lanes in the country, over the bridge. **Humber Bridge Country Park** provides a good viewing place for the bridge alongside woodland walks and the disused windmill of **Cliff Mill**, a former 'whiting mill' used for crushing chalk to be used in paints and putty. The village of Hessle itself, despite being almost swallowed by Hull's suburbs, retains a well-kept village green.
Burton Constable Hall Grand Elizabethan House, 2.5 miles off the Hornsea Rail Trail. 200 acres of Capability Brown parkland. Admission charge. Seasonal opening. (01964) 562400 for details.
Hornsea Sandy beach fronts promenade with traditional seaside attractions. Town centre has attractive buildings and local services. **Museum of Village Life** on main street. Open in summer (01964) 533443.
Hornsea Mere is Yorkshire's largest freshwater lake. Bird reserve plus boating and fishing.

INFORMATION FILE

Tourist Information

Hull 1 Paragon St (just off Victoria Sq) (01482) 223559. There is also an office at King George Dock (01482) 702118

Hornsea 75 Newbegin (01964) 536404. Seasonal opening.

Hospital Hull Royal Infirmary, Anlaby Road (01482) 328541

Banks All major banks with cashpoints are on or around Whitefriargate precinct area and Victoria Square in Hull. Newbegin (main street), Hornsea has Halifax with Link machine and Natwest with cashpoint.

⬦ **Steering Wheel Cycle Centre**, 1101-1107 Hessle High Road, Hessle (01482) 564708. **Blazing Saddles**, Unit 6, Savile St, Hull (01482) 649691 Secure cycle parking. **Freetown**, 70-80 Prospect St (01482) 589066. **Bobs Bikes**, 23 Princes Avenue, Hull (01482) 445416. **Kingston Cycles**, 245 Hessle Rd, Hull (01482) 328832. **The Cycle Shop**, 59 Southgate, Hornsea (01964) 532650.

Docks Museum, Hull town centre (section 10)

FOR ACCOMMODATION SYMBOLS KEY SEE INSIDE COVER

Boating at Hornsea Mere (section 10)

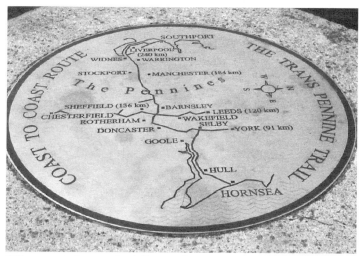

TPT monument plaque, trail end, Hornsea. Check how far you have come! (section 10)

HULL ATTRACTIONS (Map numbers refer to entries below)

• Hull sits on a spectacular river confluence, where the **River Hull** joins the **River Humber.** Its official title was granted in 1299 when Edward I gave a charter to the port and it became Kinges town upon Hull. This evolved to Kingston upon Hull.

• Take a stroll alongside the **River Hull**, lined with old warehouses and still home to river barges and coasters. It meets the Humber at an unusual looking **tidal barrier**, which protects the centre from flooding in the event of a tidal surge.

The Deep (10) Visitor attraction based on the story of the World's Oceans, with stunning aquaria and the latest interactive displays. Dramatic, iconic building thrusts 30metres over the Humber Estuary. Pedestrian and cycle bridge link to the old town. Next to the TPT. Opening late 2001 (01482) 615776.

• **Wilberforce House (2)** on the High Street is the birthplace of the famous anti-slave trade campaigner. It is now a museum to his memory and has relics of the cruel business he helped ban, such as leg-irons, whips and chains. His **statue** stands on top of a Doric column overlooking Queens Gardens.

• The **Old Town** sits between the old dock area and the River Hull and has a fascinating blend of ancient and modern architecture. It is surprising any pre-1945 buildings survive as the city was smashed by the Luftwaffe during WWII; 7,000 of its citizens died and 92% of its houses suffered bomb damage. Its most famous street is the **Land of Green Ginger (5).** Also look out for the imposing **Holy Trinity Church (6),** the city's most impressive religious building, and **Ye Olde White Hart Inn**, an historic pub.

The **Docks** stretch for some 7 miles along the Humber's north bank and the fishing, cargo handling and passenger ferry industries make it the country's third largest port. **Victoria Pier** is a good shipping observation point. The original 18th century dock has been filled in and is now **Queens Gardens**, decorated with flower beds like many other open spaces in the city. **Princes Quay** houses a futuristic shopping centre. The **Docks Museum (8)** covers centuries of maritime history, including whaling voyages to Spitsbergen and the art scrimshaw (sailors' delicate whalebone carvings). Britain's last sidewinder trawler, **The Arctic Corsair (1)**, is moored on the River Hull and is open to the public (admission fee) whilst the **Spurn Lightship (7),** once a navigation aid on the Humber Estuary, is found in Hull Marina.

Other museums and galleries include: **Ferens Art Gallery (9),** with a range of paintings from old masters to contemporary art and the **Streetlife Transport Museum (3). The Hull & East Riding Museum (4)** traces the history, geology, archaeology and natural history of the area. **(2),(3),(4),(8)** and **(9)** are open daily and admission is free. (01482) 613902. The **Yorkshire Water Museum**, Springhead Av. Willerby Rd. (01482) 652283. The star is the beam engine. Fri to Sunday 1pm to 5pm.

FREETOWN WAY

JARRAT ST

FERENSWAY

GEORGE ST

HIGH ST

DRYPOOL BRIDGE

QUEENS GARDENS

COLLIER ST

GELDER ST

i 8

VICT SQ

PARAGON ST

ALFRED

2
3

RAILWAY STATION

ANLABY RD

CARR LANE 9

ANNE ST

WHITEFRIARGATE

5

LONGATE

4

OLD TOWN

RIVER HULL

1

OSBORNE ST

PRINCES QUAY

6

MARKET

PLACE

7

CASTLE ST (A30)

HULL MARINA

HUMBER DOCK ST

QUEEN ST

10

TIDAL BARRIER

HESSLE RD (A63)

RIVER HUMBER

HULL CENTRE ATTRACTIONS

Barges on the River Hull (section 10)

HORSE STABLING FACILITIES

The following should provide horse stabling, subject to availability. Please call in advance.

Formby Hall Farm, Southport Old Road, Formby (01704) 834740. Possible stabling for one or two horses maximum.
Brook Cottage, Kay Lane, Lymm WA13 0TN (01925) 755530
For accommodation entry see page 20.
Bollington Hall Farm, Little Bollington, Altrincham WA14 4TJ
(0161) 9281760   For accommodation entry see page 20.
Manchester Equestrian Centre, Torbay Road, Urmston, Manchester M41 9WL
(0161) 7484374 / 0976 353285
High Gate Hill Equestrian Centre, Charlesworth, Glossop, SK13 9JL
(01457) 865518
Rocky's Ranch, Townhead, Dunford Bridge S36 4TG (01226) 767315
Stable facilities and pony trekking along the TPT.
Joy Cooper, Penistone Riding Club, Tanyard Farm, Oxspring
(01226) 764133 / 765919 Also very helpful if no availability to put you in touch with other stabling providers in the area.
Mallard House, Finkle Street, Wortley, S35 7DH (0114) 2888031 / 2887743
Stabling, riding school and livery near the trail.
Silkstone Equestrian Centre, Throstle Nest, Silkstone Common (01226)
790422 / 790497. Saddlery shop only (stabling in emergencies only).
Greensprings Touring Park, Rockley Abbey Farm, Rockley Lane, Worsbrough,
Barnsley S75 3DS (01226) 288298   For camping entry see page 34.
Mill Lane Stables, Mill Lane, Brayton, Selby YO8 9LB (01757) 702940
Naburn Grange Riding Centre, Naburn, York YO19 4RU (01904) 728283
Holyrood House, Hull Road, Skirlaugh, Hull HU11 5AE (01964) 562154

Help Us Keep Up to Date

New B&Bs, campsites and hostels will no doubt develop along the course of the Trans Pennine Trail. If you come across any such places not listed in this guide, or any listings that are no longer in business, please let us know. Write, phone, fax or e-mail us, using the details given at the front of the book. The most helpful communications will get a free guide of their choice; see page 80 for our current range.

INDEX
MAIN SETTLEMENTS ON THE TPT